Trⵏ
an

INTRODUCING SOCIAL POLICY
Series Editor: David Gladstone

Transport, Environment and Society

Michael Cahill

 Open University Press

Open University Press
McGraw-Hill Education
McGraw-Hill House
Shoppenhangers Road
Maidenhead
Berkshire
England
SL6 2QL

email: enquiries@openup.co.uk
world wide web: www.openup.co.uk

and Two Penn Plaza, New York, NY 10121-2289, USA

First published 2010

A catalogue record of this book is available from the British Library

ISBN13: 978 0 335 21872 1 (pb)   978 0 335 21873 8 (hb)
ISBN10: 0 335 21872 5 (pb)   0 335 21873 3 (hb)

Library of Congress Cataloging-in-Publication Data
CIP data has been applied for

Typeset by RefineCatch Ltd, Bungay, Suffolk
Printed in the UK by Bell and Bain Ltd, Glasgow

Mixed Sources
Product group from well-managed
forests and other controlled sources
www.fsc.org Cert no. TT-COC-002769
© 1996 Forest Stewardship Council

FSC

The *McGraw·Hill* Companies

For Daniel and Oliver, Joe, Ben and Chloë, Thomas and Grace

Contents

Boxes

Figures and tables

Series editor's foreword

Welcome to the eleventh volume in the Introducing Social Policy series. The series itself is designed to provide a range of well informed texts on a variety of topics that fall within the ambit of social policy studies.

Although primarily designed with undergraduate social policy students in mind, it is hoped that the series – and individual titles within it – will have a wider appeal to students in other social science disciplines and to those engaged on professional and post-qualifying courses in health care and social welfare.

The aim throughout the planning of the series has been to produce a series of texts that both reflect and contribute to contemporary thinking and scholarship, and which present their discussion in a readable and easily accessible format.

Reading Michael Cahill's book reminded me of a conversation I had about twenty years ago with a lady in a Devon village. Then aged 90, the furthest she had travelled during her long life was to Exeter, a distance of about 25 miles. Even then, her experience was singular, even unique: for it is mobility that has become the defining characteristic of the past half century. The dramatic rise in car ownership, the transportation of goods by road, as well as the availability of cheap air travel in an increasingly competitive market, have all created the means for the taken-for-granted movement from place to place that has transformed the lived experience of people in countries worldwide.

It is the growth in road transport – especially the car – which is central to this timely and important study. In it Michael Cahill develops ideas he first outlined in *The New Social Policy* published over a decade ago. Over the past fifty years the transition from public to private transport has not only transformed the lives of those who drive and use a car, in convenience, accessibility and opportunity, it has also had a significant impact on our built environment in terms of land-use planning, urban design and community living. But there are other consequences of this transport revolution: not least in terms of ill-health and obesity, disabling traffic accidents, the social exclusion of non-drivers and the impact on disabled and older people of a reduced and restricted system of public transport. The balance sheet, of course, has also to be set within the parameters of public policy and against the mounting environmental concern with carbon emissions, which are generated especially by the transport sector.

In *Transport, Environment and Society*, Michael Cahill takes us well beyond social policy's traditional preoccupation with the 'five giants' of the classic welfare state, and makes a stimulating contribution to a broader understanding of welfare as well-being. In that sense, too, as well as the subject matter of his book, it is a tract for the times.

David Gladstone
University of Bristol

Acknowledgements

I first discussed many of the issues which surround the car in the 1960s and 1970s with my father who, as an ex-cyclist, was saddened and angry at what planners were doing to the city of Portsmouth to accommodate the car. Our discussions enabled me to see from my teenage years the damage that cars do to the environment and society.

Since we first met in 1986 my wife Vanessa Cahill has put up with far too many conversations about the car and society. Without her willingness to read successive drafts this would be a poorer text. It would also not be as informed, as she has given me many examples from her professional practice as a social worker with older and disabled people.

Thanks to the following who have read and commented upon various chapters: Maria Antoniou, Derrick Coffee, Ben Fincham, Stephanie Fleischer, Lesley Murray, Graham Sharp.

I was able to complete the book with the help of the School of Applied Social Science, University of Brighton who awarded me a sabbatical semester. I am also indebted to the inter-library loans staff at the University's Falmer library, and to Kimberley Gray and Toby Leyton for their help.

David Gladstone has been an admirable editor, patient and supportive throughout.

In a book of this kind, drawing on many sources, there are bound to be some errors and inaccuracies for which I apologize in advance.

Michael Cahill

Connections: transport, environment and social policy

It has been my experience that students of social science are not attracted to the topic of transport. Why that it is the case I am not actually sure. Perhaps it conjures up pictures of an obsession with engines, the Highway Code and trainspotting? To dismiss such an interest as nerdiness ignores the fact that engineering is vital for the running of a modern society, traffic requires rules and regulations and, yes, for many people there is a fascination in watching railway engines. This book, however, is about the human consequences of our transport system, with chapters on stages in the life course, from childhood to old age, relating to the transport system and questions of mobility. The car is the focus of the book because it has transformed social life and our environment and society over the past half century in a way that no other transport technology has. Transport is interpreted broadly and includes walking as well as movement in and by machines, be they bicycles, buses, trains, cars or planes. Discussion of the environment in this book relates to the local environment so that long-distance transport is not covered here.

The connections between transport and social policy are explored through an examination of the social implications of the way in which transport is organized and the transport implications of the way in which social policy is organized. The book explores the social and environmental implications of transport policy and transport choices.

Transport is an essential component of a modern economy and society where goods have to be moved and people need to travel. Economies based on exporting and importing goods are reliant on systems of transportation which are an important part of the infrastructure of society. Trading has been a feature of civilizations for millennia but there has never been so much trade, travel and mobility as in the contemporary world. In rich world societies social life is premised on the assumption of mobility – to meet one another, to go to work, to shop, to go on holiday. Transport technology has had a considerable impact over the past century on the economy and society. The invention of the internal combustion engine at the end of the nineteenth century was to have incalculable economic, environmental and social consequences. As has the invention of the jet engine, a product of the 1930s, which meant that by the late twentieth century air transport was a key factor in the emergence of a global society.

Mobility

Mobility – the ability to travel, to move from place to place – is a taken-for-granted aspect of contemporary society where it can be as commonplace as the journey to work or as exotic as a holiday in the Seychelles.

Greatly increased personal mobility is conventionally seen as a form of liberation, of release from the boundaries of place and an exercise of personal freedom which adds to international understanding as well as individual happiness. In the contemporary world, mobility is all-pervasive, it is routine for large numbers of people to travel to other countries for business or holidays, while economic migrants travel in search of work.

Mobility has a positive connotation: many people speak of being 'free to move' and delight in the freedom that certain forms of transport – pre-eminently cars – give them. To move is an achievement: a toddler's first steps are a milestone in his or her development. Similarly, in old age the inability to walk or to get out of one's chair unaided are signs of physical decline. But we can also be mobile without moving our bodies – the telephone and the computer enable communication across the globe. Technological advances mean that mobile phones together with other aspects of information and communication technology (ICT) give certain office workers the ability to work away from the office – whether they are travelling on a train or staying at a hotel or working from home. We live in an era in which ICT has transformed daily life: 'virtual mobility' has arrived, as many journeys are now redundant because of the use of computers linked to the Internet. It is now possible for people in different countries to communicate and send documents easily using the World Wide Web. This has the potential to reduce travelling and to reduce the number of journeys, which are thought necessary. As the world takes carbon reduction more seriously then we can expect that much more extensive use will be made of this technology.

Time and motion

One of the remarkable features of the contemporary world is the way in which time has been 'compressed' along with space. Distances have been reduced because of developments in technology which have made travelling easier. The rise of rail, car and air travel has reduced distance and brought people closer to one another. It has also meant that migration has been made easier with movements of peoples around and across the world.

International trade has been a major beneficiary of this process with a world market now existing in many goods. This might be said to have begun with the discovery of the Americas by Christopher Columbus in 1492 when the New World was opened up by the Spanish and then the Portuguese, Dutch and British. This travel was sea based and the ships certainly reduced time and space.

Time is today a major factor in relation to individual and collective decision making in transport. Part of the justification for major road building schemes is that they will reduce journey times and hence improve the efficiency of the economy. One of the reasons why it is so difficult to persuade many people of the attractions of more sustainable modes of transport than the car – walking, cycling or public transport – is that unfavourable comparisons are made with the time it takes to travel by car. Time-saving travelling for one group can mean that another group has to spend more time travelling. Some public transport journeys can take inordinate amounts of time with the result that they are sometimes not attempted. The relocation of depots and facilities on the outskirts of towns and cities so that lorries can reach them easily means that journeys to them on foot can take significant amounts of time. This represents a redistribution of time – the business saves time but imposes time costs on the user of the service.

Social policy and transport

Social policy can be said to be about the ways in which men and women can achieve the choices and the opportunities which they desire to attain a good life (Dean 2006). Social policy as the promotion of human welfare and well-being, encompasses more than the study of welfare state services, although it has an obvious focus on them. I have argued this case in *The New Social Policy* where one of the chapters was devoted to transport (Cahill 1994). The present book affords me the opportunity to pursue some of the topics outlined in that chapter in much greater depth. One of the premises of *The New Social Policy* was that social, economic and technological change had created a vastly different society from that of the period 1945–75, the era of the 'classic welfare state' in which the academic study of social policy and administration emerged in the UK. I argued that welfare and well-being had to be analysed in a consumer society in which individualized self-interest was eroding an older ethic of care and citizenship. Allied with novel technological developments this exacerbated the disadvantage of many people, creating new categories of deprivation such as the 'information poor' and the 'transport poor'. At the same time, subjective well-being was influenced by the persuasion techniques of consumer society and the media attention given to the super-rich to acquire consumer durables in the search for the good life. There has been accumulating evidence, however, that consumption-based lifestyles did not automatically enhance feelings of individual well-being. Indeed, individualization seemed to damage important social relationships and the experience of community (Offer 2006; Searle 2008). Much of the economic change centred on the creation of networks which facilitate the speedy transmission of goods, services and people. The dominant political interpretation of these changes was that they led inevitably to deregulation, privatization and free markets. The way we travel and organize transport has been profoundly affected by these shifts in political thought and, as we will see, it has in its turn led to a deterioration in neighbourhood and community life.

Making the connections between transport and social policy is not a straightforward exercise. Indeed, some might argue that transport issues are not within the province of social policy. To those who, like Spicker (2008), argue that social policy and administration should not encompass the subject matter of this book, there are a number of responses. Welfare state services are nowadays organized and delivered in a mobility-dependent society. Issues of accessibility are at the forefront of government transport policy and it is acknowledged, certainly since the publication of the social exclusion report on public transport, that they have cross-department implications (Social Exclusion Unit 2003). Health, education, employment, social care, all are encouraged by government to work in an integrated manner. Dimensions of social need and issues of social welfare are to be found within the study of transport and mobility: obesity, physical activity, the journey to school are examples. Policy interdependence has been a feature of government for some time, and since Labour came to power in 1997 this has become much more explicit. The government's first White Paper on transport policy was imbued with 'joined up' thinking, hence its title *A New Deal for Transport* (Department of the Environment, Transport and the Regions 1998) echoing the famous twentieth-century programme of social and economic change, the New Deal of President Roosevelt in the 1930s. The *New Deal for Transport* announced the government's belief that the transport system should be fair, accessible and form part of the government's sustainable development strategy. Its call for an integrated transport policy implied that transport objectives should be coordinated with other policy areas. This had been obvious for some years. Transport has become so important in the contemporary world that its presence or absence has implications for employment, health, housing and social care. A lack of access to transport can prevent people from turning up for a hospital appointment, constrain their choice of job and limit where they can live. This becomes a bigger problem each year as more of the adult population become car drivers and local public transport further declines as a result. Finally, social policy interest has never been solely in the administration and management of agencies but also in more intangible, yet important, issues such as citizenship, community, equality of opportunity, and social justice, all of which have clear mobility and transport components.

Environmental impacts of transport

We now know, as previous generations did not, that there are serious environmental consequences resulting from the widespread use of cars and aeroplanes. Transport has far-reaching environmental implications: 28 per cent of the UK's carbon emissions come from transport journeys (Royal Commission on Environmental Pollution 2007: 18). The transport sector in the UK is the third largest cause of carbon dioxide emissions (Bristow et al. 2004: 3). Worldwide there are now over 750 million cars. These vehicles have many environmental impacts: transport pollutes the air, takes up vast areas of land in the shape of motorways and other major roads, land for parking, land for petrol stations and other auto-oriented businesses. As the overwhelming majority (97 per cent) of motor vehicles use oil, carbon emissions in transport are a major problem. Oil is a finite resource and there are estimates that world stocks will be largely depleted by 2050 (Black and Nijkamp 2000: 141). The contribution of aircraft to climate change is much smaller at present but, given the expansion plans announced by the government and with air travel forecast to grow year on year, aircraft will produce a major proportion of UK carbon emissions, wiping out the savings made in other areas. Flying is a very carbon intensive activity not only because the oil-based fuel, kerosene, produces prodigious amounts of carbon but also because planes fly at altitudes which ensure that the pollution is even more damaging than were it to be on the ground.

The UK government has given the go-ahead to airports all over the country to expand the number of flights that they handle. Currently 200 million people pass through UK airports, but the government's White Paper on aviation published in 2003 forecast as many as 400 million people passing through UK airports by 2020 and 500 million by 2030 (Department for Transport 2003a). Growth in air travel affects the environment locally through noise, air pollution, and damage to wildlife, heritage and landscapes. Emissions from aircraft engines contribute to global warming but they also damage the upper atmosphere. Hillman and Fawcett (2004: 150) point out that 'each kilometer covered by air within Europe accounts for around two and a half times the equivalent carbon dioxide emissions of the same distance by car (and around five times those by train)'.

With the government now accepting that the UK needs to make cuts of 80 per cent in carbon emissions by 2050, the projected growth in aviation seems like policy schizophrenia. Aviation is an industry which has extensive state aid and currently enjoys a special status: 'it benefits from no taxation on fuel, spin off research and development from military developments and generous assistance with new airports and surface transport infrastructure' (Whitelegg and Cambridge 2004: 8). Moreover, it is not just the carbon emissions from aircraft which damage the environment, for nitrous oxides, soot and water vapour released at different heights add to the warming effect (Bows and Anderson 2007: 103). Cheap air travel has enabled large numbers of people to holiday in many parts of Europe and significant numbers of Brits to purchase second homes in sunnier climes. Ruth Kelly MP, when she was Transport Secretary, argued for the democratizing influence of air travel: 'We all cherish the opportunity to visit friends and family abroad, catch up with loved ones, or take a well earned holiday. But if we want to maintain those hard-won opportunities, I truly believe we must be brave in challenging those who would ration flying and make it once more the preserve of the rich' (Kelly 2008). Yet survey evidence shows people from the top three social classes take on average more than four times as many flights in a year as those in the bottom three social classes (Bishop and Grayling 2003: 64). The *National Travel Survey 2007* reports: 'In 2007 25 per cent of those in the lowest income households had made an international flight in the last 12 months, compared with 71 per cent of those in the highest income households' (Department for Transport 2008b).

Government policy on aviation still appears to operate with a 'predict and provide' approach, seeing it as vital for economic competitiveness in a global economy.

Low-cost airlines have transformed flying into a mass activity and there has been a major increase in the number of air passengers. This has been very important for opening up many destinations as holiday spots and expanded the travel horizons of many people. Yet 75 per cent of those who use budget airlines are in social classes A, B and C, while people with second homes abroad take an average of six return flights a year. Most of the growth, the government envisages, will take place among the wealthiest 10 per cent (Civil Aviation Authority cited in Bishop and Grayling 2003: 64).

Cars do not produce as much pollution as they did a decade ago because of the fitting of catalytic converters and the cleaner engines that motor manufacturers provide. However, this does not mean that the overall amount of pollution from motor vehicles has reduced – on the contrary it has increased. This is because the number of vehicles on the roads has grown, and continues to grow each year. In 2004 there were 32.3 million licensed vehicles on the roads of which 80 per cent were private cars (Office for National Statistics 2005).

Noise pollution from motor vehicles is another growing environmental problem which results from this. 'Traffic noise accounts for 66% of the total noise generated outside dwellings in the UK, with 32 million people being exposed to high levels of noise (55–75 decibels)' (UK Noise Association 2007). There are some parts of the country – for example, the south east of England – where it is difficult to find a location which is not within earshot of vehicle noise. There are ways of reducing this noise pollution – different road surfaces for example – but this can be outweighed by the increase in the number of vehicles. Some 'road improvements' can merely move the problem. Bypasses have been the traffic engineers' preferred way of dealing with overcrowded roads through the centres of towns and villages, but these can result in increased noise levels for those who are unfortunate enough to live adjacent to the bypass.

Visual pollution from motor vehicles is much less remarked upon but is nonetheless apparent. No one confronted with a vista across a large car park can claim that it is a beautiful sight. Thousands of car parks have been built in towns and cities since 1945. The Victorians bequeathed us an invaluable legacy of public parks whereas our gift to future generations has been car parks. Similarly, in streets with heavy parking on both sides of the road the vehicles clutter and disfigure the architecture and public space.

Vehicle pollution can be particularly hazardous for certain groups in the population: those with respiratory conditions, and those with immature lungs (children). Many urban areas are high pollution spots, and certain weather conditions exacerbate the pollution and its impact: for example, if there is heavy low cloud cover then the pollution cannot escape and it stays close to the ground. Another pollutant which has adverse effects on human health is ozone, but PM10s are the major killer among the noxious substances which come out of exhaust pipes. These are the microscopically small particles which are to be found in diesel fuel. The latest estimate is that their existence leads to at least 24,000 premature deaths a year (Royal Commission on Environmental Pollution 2007).

The environmental consequences of our oil-dependent way of life are now plain to see with the impact of human-induced climate change. Climate change is going to affect rich and poor, young and old. Yet the people of the rich world are better able to protect themselves, and the worst effects will be seen in the poor world as severe weather conditions and rising sea levels create death, destruction and millions of refugees. Nonetheless, within rich-world countries the poorest will also be disproportionately affected by climate change. Reducing carbon emissions will require that all sections of transport play a part. There are questions of global justice involved here, for climate change has had its worst impacts so far on people living in the poor world. As Roberts and Parks (2007: 9) summarize the position:

> The existing body of scientific evidence on global climate change strongly suggests that the emissions coming out of our exhaust pipes

contribute to a layer of heat-trapping carbon dioxide that will create – and perhaps has already created – a warmer and wetter atmosphere, and, in turn, terrible outcomes like more flooding in Bangladesh, devastating hurricanes in the Caribbean, and droughts in the Sudano-Sahel region of Africa.

We automatically think of the 'big picture' topics, such as climate change, when we hear the word 'environment' and this can lead us to forget the stresses and strains which the transport system puts on the local environment outside our own front door. Take a walk down the street where you live and you will notice all sorts of impacts which are the result of traffic. Naturally, if you live in an area with heavy traffic then there is the pollution which you can smell as you breathe, but take a look at those cracks to the pavement caused by cars driven on to the pavement, the noise of passing traffic, the broken kerb stones, the van parked right across the pavement so that people have to walk in the road, the low number of people walking down the street. Again, we often think of environment as meaning nature, but for many people – often those on low incomes or social security – the environment surrounding their house or flat is not one of trees, lawns and gardens but treeless streets with high volumes of traffic. These are environmental and social consequences of the way we travel.

Accessibility

Physical accessibility has to be considered in transport: how easy or how difficult is it for people to reach certain destinations? With the widespread assumption that all adults are able to drive cars, inequality of access has increased, meaning that those people who do not drive find that their ability to participate in society is reduced.

The car affords drivers a flexibility, a 'go anywhere at any time' ability which public transport cannot match (Urry 2007: 190–4).

The UK is a car-dependent society where it is often necessary to have a car in order to reach the doctor's surgery, the local hospital or to access local services. Those who do not have access to a car are at a disadvantage and this can affect the take-up of services. Paid employment is now seen by governments as important in getting people off social security and in enhancing self-esteem, yet the decentralizaton of employment to out-of-town industrial estates and office parks over the past twenty years makes it more difficult for non-motorists to reach the jobs available. These locations are designed with cars in mind – their large car parks attest to this. Bus services cannot provide an adequate service to these locations, designed as they were for the convenience of the car not the bus. Many post-war housing estates, too, have been built with the assumption that residents will have access to a car. The population density of some estates is just too low to support a bus service.

In his famous and oft-quoted essay on citizenship T. H. Marshall introduced the concept of social rights to denote the services and benefits which the welfare state provided after 1948 (Marshall and Bottomore 1992). As has been suggested, access to health, housing and employment is more difficult – indeed, sometimes impossible – for those without access to the car. In our time, unlike in 1950 when Marshall gave his lectures on which his essay is based, citizenship means being able to access services. Without this ability the carless become 'second class citizens' (Urry 2007). Social policy displays a commitment to the improvement of life for those who are denied opportunities through age, race, gender or disability, so lack of mobility fits into this schema. Feelings are important as well in day-to-day travelling. Waiting for long periods at bus stops for buses which never arrive, having to leave events by a certain time, being unable to enjoy a social life because there is no evening bus all leave their mark on the individual. Some of this is to do with comparisons with other people who are car owners; much is to do with feeling resentful about having to wait in cold, dirty and unkempt environments. These are the 'psycho-social injuries of inequality structures' (Elstad quoted in Searle 2008: 33) which can leave people feeling that they are not as important as others, that society is organized around car drivers. Stress can result from this, related to the reduced degree of control that people believe that they have over their lives. The advent of mass car ownership has changed the terms on which we experience daily life. The car endows the driver with the freedom to be mobile at the time of his or her choosing, the ability to travel door to door and to travel to hitherto unreachable places. As we shall explore in this book, the individuals and households without a car see their opportunities decline as public transport is reduced and amenities become more difficult to access without a car.

One of the contentions of this book is that car dependence has reached such a high level that it is becoming increasingly difficult for carless people to enjoy the same range of choices and aspirations as their more mobile compatriots. Transport can create or deny access to a service, the mobility needed to participate in society and the means by which one's needs or the needs of one's loved ones are met. Amartya Sen (1995) has written of capabilities – what people are able to do and to be – and Nussbaum (2000) has identified functionings which go to make up capabilities (see Box 1.1). Bodily integrity is on the list alongside play, control over one's environment and bodily health. (For a full list see Wolff and De-Shalit 2007: 38–40.) Mobility is covered by the Bodily Integrity category because it involves 'being able to move freely from place to place' as well as the security of one's person and reproductive rights.

> **Box 1.1 Nussbaum's list of functionings**
>
> 1. Life: Being able to live to the end of a human life of normal length.
> 2. Bodily health: Being able to have good health.
> 3. Bodily integrity: Being able to move freely from place to place.
> 4. Sense, imagination and thought: Being able to use the senses, to imagine, think and reason.
> 5. Emotions: Being able to have attachments to things and to people outside ourselves.
> 6. Practical reason: Being able to form a conception of the good and to engage in critical reflection about the planning of one's life.
> 7. Affiliation: Being able to live with and towards others.
> 8. Other species: Being able to live with concern for and in relation to animals, plants and the world of nature.
> 9. Play: Being able to laugh, to play, to enjoy recreational activities.
> 10. Control over one's environment: Being able to participate effectively in political choices that govern one's life.
>
> *Source:* Wolff and De-Shalit 2007: 38–40.

Capabilities are what one is achieving and what one has the potential to achieve. The lack of mobility, or reduced mobility, can be said to be capability deprivation. Being able to move freely from place to place, to where one wants to go is an important freedom. Being able to choose one's means of transport is important rather than being denied choice because one does not have the money for the bus fare or being unable to reach a chosen destination because public transport does not permit it. To be denied freedom of movement, either by bodily failure or by lack of access to technology is a corrosive disadvantage, to employ the expression used by Wolff and De-Shalit, that is to say, a disadvantage the presence of which leads to further disadvantage. It should be noted that this is not arguing that all people should have the right to use all forms of transport, for that would be absurd and dangerous for individual lives and the society. Rather it implies that there needs to be a 'national minimum' of transport, to use a key term from the citizenship debate, which would enable the carless to reach destinations and permit more choice by car drivers as to how they travel. We can say that immobility is a form of capability deprivation. Mobility has become much more important and it enables us to enjoy relationships with others, to further our interests and to participate in our society.

From cradle to grave: structure and organization of the book

This book uses the perspective of social policy to highlight the ways in which contemporary social life is structured and maintained via transport. From the early 1950s through to the 1970s, the years of the long post-war boom and the 'classic welfare state', sociologists and social policy analysts ignored the ways in which cars were changing the economy and society. Sociology's engagement with the car was to examine the lives of well-paid car workers which led to the 'embourgeoisment thesis' (Goldthorpe et al. 1968) Community studies, an important part of the output of sociology in the 1950s and 1960s, largely ignored the impact of the car on the areas studied. Why sociology was 'transport blind' is an interesting question but one that need not detain us here. It was left to Ivan Illich, a maverick Roman Catholic priest, to raise questions of automobiles and equity in the mid-1970s and for the emerging environmental lobby in the UK to put cars on the agenda as a problem area (Illich 1974; but also see Hirsch 1976 and Bendixson 1977). In other words, the engagement with the social implications of mass car ownership came from outside sociology. Social policy, too, was not interested in the implications of this major social change for people's welfare until the 1990s (Cahill 1992, 1994; Jones 1996). When social policy and administration was detailing and documenting the impact of social inequality in the 1960s and 1970s one of the major social divisions emerging between car drivers and the carless was ignored.

One must bear in mind, however, that public transport in the UK was, until the 1970s, still part of the social democratic alternative to individual private ownership, along with public housing and comprehensive education. In those years transport could still be written about as a social service, but the Conservative Party after Mrs Thatcher became leader in 1975 was clear that it wanted to create not only a property-owning democracy but a car-owning one as well. There is now cross party consensus on this. Chapters 2 and 3 explore the structure and organization of transport policy as well as the changing political ideologies around mass car ownership and their social and environmental consequences.

Chapter 4 discusses the risks of life, death and serious injury from the transport system and then examines the health-enhancing modes of walking and cycling and their contribution to a healthy life. The government and local authorities in the UK have for some fifteen years been engaged in public education campaigns to get people out of their cars and walking and cycling. With a few exceptions – such as increased bus patronage in Brighton and London – this has been unsuccessful. Indeed, the trends are going the other way: larger vehicles such as 4 × 4s are becoming more popular, motorists are travelling longer distances and car dependence is more entrenched. Physical exercise has been taken out of transport for many motorists because car travel is a sedentary form of transport. Its growing popularity since the early 1950s in the UK has meant that active forms of transport – walking and cycling – have been in decline. Figures reveal that only one in five of the UK population exercise for 30 minutes a day five days a week which is the Department of Health's recommendation for adults (*Guardian*,

8 December 2006). Chapter 4 examines the recent evidence on the relationship between our health and the way we travel.

The book uses a lifecycle approach to show how transport and mobility options are important throughout our lives from cradle to grave. Social policy is involved with the successive phases of our lives from childhood, through adulthood to retirement and old age, with services and benefits designed for these different life stages. Transport affects each of these structuring the opportunities which will be available to each person in their life.

The focus is on one transport mode, the car, because it has made such a big difference to everyday life. The car assumes such importance because it is a personal and private vehicle, emblematic of a consumer society which not only embodies the consumer virtues of choice and independence but has had profound impacts on the look, design and feel of so many neighbourhoods. Chapter 5 examines the ways in which this technology has changed adult lives, both men and women.

Chapter 6 is about all those other adults who either choose not to drive, cannot drive because of a disability or simply cannot afford to drive a car and rely on walking, cycling and public transport or lifts from other people to get around. Now that the study of poverty has broadened its focus it is recognized that lack of transport can lead to serious social exclusion both for individuals and for communities. Across a wide range of areas of modern life people assume that others will have cars ('your own transport') and much of modern life is built around this assumption. Chapter 6 explores the many facets of social exclusion and transport.

For many teenagers the onset of adulthood is symbolized by gaining a driving licence. The responsibility which this gives a 17-year-old seems to signify that childhood is at an end, no longer will they have to rely on their parents for a lift. In the lifecycle organization of this book the chapter on drivers (Chapter 6) is about adulthood and transport, in particular the differing experiences of men and women.

The car-based transport system has meant that children get much less opportunity to play on the streets than did their forebears, for their parents – rightly in many cases – judge it to be too dangerous. Likewise, although the great majority of children own a bicycle, they do not use it for personal transport as the roads have become too dangerous. This has affected not only children's physical development but also their social and psychological development.

Children's independent mobility has been severely curtailed by the motorization of society. It has meant that it is perceived to be no longer safe to play in the street with the consequence that many children now live much more home-centred lives than previous generations as their parents are fearful that they will come to harm if they use the streets as play space. This is particularly damaging for children's physical health, as many of them are not getting the exercise which they require for the healthy development of their bodies. Chapter 7 explores how children's lives are affected by transport.

Mobility has a particular resonance for many disabled people for it is what they aspire to but are often denied because of their physical disability. Disabled people in England and Wales travel one-third less than the non-disabled public (Wilson 2003). Surveys reveal that transport is a very important issue for them. Chapter 8 explores the difficulties and opportunities presented by the organization of the transport system for disabled people.

Some older people are also among those who have been adversely affected by transport trends. Many of the problems are the same as those experienced by disabled people, indeed, two-thirds of disabled people are over retirement age. Just as for teenagers the gaining of the driving licence is a form of independence, so the decision to give up that licence can seem like a loss of independence. Cars are extraordinarily useful if you cannot walk very far, cannot carry heavy loads and live some distance from the nearest shop. The position of older people – drivers and non-drivers – is reviewed and government policy on their transport needs is discussed in Chapter 9.

As we have noted, the academic study of social policy was slow to acknowledge the impact of the car on its subject matter. This book makes the case that social policy needs to foreground issues of access and mobility. Social policy has prided itself on articulating the experiences and perspectives of those who receive and use services. These dilemmas need to be related to some of the key themes of social policy analysis. The final chapter shows how some core concerns of social policy, particularly its recent attention to social justice, are central to the study of transport and mobility and will become increasingly so. Furthermore, the themes introduced in this book are also a matter of environmental justice and sustainable development and the final chapter returns to making connections between transport, environment and society. Measures adopted to combat global warming will mean a serious consideration of the extent to which the car-dependent lifestyle can continue. If mobility and travelling are seriously questioned then the locality becomes much more important and this connects with the rethinking of food production if 'food miles' are taken into account, the extent to which clothing should rely on poor-world cheap labour and the viability of local production.

There needs to be a greater integration of environmental, social and transport policy if a fairer and sustainable transport policy is to emerge. Policy needs to respond much more than it has done to the lived experience of those who use our transport system. Transport shapes society but society shapes transport (Lyons 2003). The next chapter investigates the way in which transport policy in the UK has developed and explores the necessary conditions for a sustainable transport system.

Further reading

Dean, H. (2006). *Social Policy*. Cambridge: Polity Press. An introduction to social policy as the study of human well-being.

Urry, J. (2007). *Mobilities*. Cambridge: Polity Press. The best source for an exposition of the 'mobilities paradigm' in social science.

two

Policies, politics and protests

Over the past forty years transport has from time to time become a 'hot' political issue, as in 2000 when fuel protests saw the government become very unpopular as petrol pumps ran dry and a state of emergency was declared. In some part, this was the expression of the sentiment that motorists are unfairly treated by governments. In fact, as we shall see, it has been the growing environmental consciousness from the 1960s which has been behind many of the political controversies surrounding transport: in the 1960s there was opposition in many cities to the road building programme as it was felt that communities and neighbourhoods were being destroyed. Subsequently, environmental pollution by the car has led to campaigning activity from many quarters, while in the 1990s there were numerous battles at construction sites where new roads were being built in unspoilt countryside. There has been a backlash to this with increasing numbers of motorists believing that they are being unfairly pilloried. Meanwhile local newspapers would be short of news if there were not a continuing supply of stories around parking issues usually involving local authorities. Transport is a regular source of stories for the national papers as well with the tabloids frequently taking up the cause of the motorist or the harassed commuter against the supposed unfair treatment meted out to them. None of this should surprise us, for along with the weather one's journey is a fixed topic of conversation in daily life.

To understand the context in which transport plays such an important part in our lives it is necessary to know something of the structure and function of transport policy making in the UK. The first part of this chapter provides an introduction to the political bodies responsible for transport policy in this country while the second part is a brief guide to the contemporary history of transport policy: the campaigns, the issues, the key decisions, the White Papers which shape the ways in which we discuss transport issues today and determine how decisions are made.

Central government

The Department for Transport, although an important ministry, is not one of the great offices of state. Despite the fact that the Secretary of State for Transport is a member of the Cabinet, the office does not hold the same cachet for politicians as other spending ministries such as Education, Health or Work and Pensions. Like them it does, however, affect us all directly as when we step outside our front door, in the shape of road design, the Highway Code, speed limits and street layout. Today the Department for Transport is concerned with the formulation and implementation of national transport policy but it has lost its service delivery role to the Highways Agency – an 'arm's length agency' to which the Department for Transport has entrusted the day-to-day running of the A roads and motorways and the responsibility for building major new roads. The Highways Agency is an executive agency of the Department for Transport. Ninety per cent of the staff of the Department for Transport work in these agencies, which cover, as well as highways, driver licensing, transport research and the vehicle inspectorate (Glaister et al. 2006: 47). However, the crucial (political) decision-making power as to which roads are built remains with the Department.

In Scotland, Wales and Northern Ireland powers over bus services, motorways, other roads, rail and land-use planning have been devolved to the national bodies, while the Department for Transport retains control over international transport, safety issues, vehicle licensing and certain other areas. Since devolution this has led to different emphases in the various regions, as in Scotland where free bus travel for all aged over 60 was introduced before the rest of the UK and subsidies are given to air and ferry services to the Scottish islands (Docherty et al. 2007: 142). In both Scotland and Wales there has been a move away from the priority of sustainable transport to transport as stimulating and supporting economic development (Mackinnon and Vigar in Docherty and Shaw 2008: 44).

When the Ministry of Transport was created in 1919 its major role was the oversight of the rail system which was still in private ownership. Railways had been the new technology of transport in the nineteenth century, transforming economic and social life by linking distant towns and cities, reducing time spent on journeys and providing an infrastructure for the transport of goods in the economy (Wolmar 2007). Railways were still the major mode of transport at the formation of the Ministry in 1919. There was some heated debate as to whether they should be brought under national control – nationalized – and whether there should be a separate ministry for the railways (Plowden 1971). Rail nationalization had to wait until 1947 when the Ministry in effect became responsible for the running of the railways via British Railways.

The motor car transformed economic and social life in twentieth-century Britain as railways had done in the nineteenth. The number of cars on the roads greatly increased in the inter-war period. Yet cars were not the only application of the internal combustion engine: motor buses and coaches provided new transport opportunities for millions of people: 'Never before had the British public travelled so frequently and so regularly as in the years between the wars' (Dyos and Aldcroft 1973: 373). If the impact of motor transport on social life was apparent it also had a major influence on economic life, as by the end of the 1930s it was estimated that between 1.3 million and 1.5 million people were employed in vehicle manufacture, operation or servicing (Dyos and Aldcroft 1973: 370). For most of this time the Ministry had the responsibility for trunk roads (A roads) and, from the 1950s, for motorways as well. Over the years the Ministry of Transport became in effect a Ministry for Roads, and the bias continues to the present day with most staff being employed on roads issues.

When Labour returned to power in 1997 transport became part of a merged 'super-ministry' designed to integrate transport and environmental policy: the Department of the Environment, Transport and the Regions (DETR). The new government's approach to transport policy was announced in the 1998 White Paper *A New Deal for Transport*. This set out an integrated transport policy heralding an emphasis on promoting public transport together with the more sustainable modes of cycling and walking. Labour governments had been proponents of integrated transport for some considerable time; in the 1970s, when they were last in power, most of public transport was under public control but what they inherited in 1997 from the Conservatives was a denationalized railway and bus industry. Within the *New Deal for Transport* there was a discussion of the ways in which people could be persuaded to use their cars less and other modes more. A great many of these ideas were to surface in the Transport Act 2000, including road pricing and workplace car park charging. The new Labour government committed itself to a policy of road traffic reduction and expansion of public transport.

Box 2.1 Department for Transport strategic objectives

1. To sustain economic growth and improved productivity through reliable and efficient transport networks

- Journey time on main roads in urban areas.
- Journey time reliability on the strategic road network, as measured by the average delay experienced in the worst 10 per cent of journeys for each monitored route.
- Level of capacity and crowding on the rail network.
- Reliability on the rail network as measured by the 'public performance measure' (PPM).

- Average benefit/cost ratio of investments approved over the Comprehensive Spending Review 2007 period.

2. **To improve the environmental performance of transport and tackle climate change**

- Develop a carbon reduction strategy for transport.
- Agree an improved EU Emissions Trading Scheme for the post-2012 period that includes aviation.
- Introduce the Renewable Transport Fuels Obligation – requiring 5 per cent of all UK fuel sold on UK forecourts to come from a renewable source by 2010.
- Introduce successor arrangements to the voluntary agreements with car manufacturers on new car CO_2.
- Progress towards meeting the Air Quality Strategy objectives for eight air pollutants as illustrated by trends in measurements of two of the more important pollutants which affect public health: particles and nitrogen dioxide (led by Defra).

3. **To strengthen the safety and security of transport**

- Reduce the number of people killed or seriously injured in Great Britain in road accidents by 40 per cent and the number of children killed or seriously injured by 50 per cent, by 2010 compared with the average for 1994–98, tackling the significantly higher incidence in disadvantaged communities.
- Deliver Transport's contribution to the Home Office led Public Service Agreement: target to 'reduce the risk to the UK and its interests overseas from international terrorism'.

4. **To enhance access to jobs, services and social networks, including for the most disadvantaged**

- Increase the number of buses and trains accessible to disabled people.
- Increase the number of stations re/accredited under the Secure Stations Scheme by 15 per cent.
- Access to services and facilities by public transport, walking and cycling.

Source: Department for Transport strategic objectives, http://www.dft.gov.uk/about/howthedftworks/dso

The Treasury

The Treasury has a fair degree of control over Department for Transport activities given that it holds the purse strings. For example, in the Budget Report for 2008 the Chancellor made announcements on the changes to car vehicle excise duty rates, the alterations to the fuel duty rates, the taxation of company cars, measures to ensure that only the most sustainable biofuels were used and an increase in tax revenues with the new aeroplane duty. The relationship between the Treasury and the Department for Transport is not an equal one, with the former having a great deal more clout in negotiations; indeed, the Chancellor does make some key decisions on transport matters without consultation with the Department. This has been the case with the fuel duty escalator. The government has improved the nature of transport planning ending the previous short-termism with the introduction of a ten-year transport plan with spending priorities which have been agreed by the Treasury (Glaister et al. 2006: 56–7). An important part of the relationship between the Treasury and the Department are the Public Service Agreements which outline a series of policy objectives, for example on journey reliability, punctuality or rail services, increased use of buses, reduction of deaths and serious injuries from road accidents (Parkhurst and Dudley 2008).

Every major policy area has a parliamentary select committee which monitors its work and produces reports on topics relevant to the area. The Transport Select Committee scrutinizes the work of the Department via calls for written evidence, taking oral evidence and producing reports. The Committee, like all the parliamentary select committees, is composed of members from all the three main political parties.

Local authorities

Local authorities have an important role in the delivery of transport policy as they control 96 per cent of the road network (Glaister et al. 2006). One needs to be clear, however, that not all local authorities have transport responsibilities. In the larger urban areas of England, throughout Wales and Scotland, together with Greater London there are unitary authorities responsible for both planning and transport. Outside of the major urban areas in England county councils are responsible for transport and not the district councils. Central government provides the finance for the local authority's transport schemes and the ongoing costs which it has to meet: road maintenance, pavement maintenance and support for bus services which are socially useful but not economic for a bus company to run unaided. The relationship between central and local government in transport policy and planning is a long-standing one.

Our system of local government was created in the nineteenth century through a series of Acts of Parliament starting with the Municipal Corporations Act of 1835 (Fraser 1976). It does not have an existence independent of central government which can, if it chooses, abolish local authorities and amend or remove their powers.

Local authorities had the responsibility for the maintenance and construction of roads until the Ministry of Transport was established in 1919, although a Roads Board had been created in 1910 to give financial support to this work. The Ministry was created because the government decided that roads were just as much a national responsibility as railways. From 1919 to the present there has been a dual split between the Ministry and the local authorities in transport planning and the delivery of policy.

Local government is the subordinate partner in this relationship, given the financial weakness of local authorities – only one-quarter of their expenditure is raised from local taxes. Taxation on local firms, the non-domestic rate, is not collected by local authorities but by central government which then distributes it to local authorities on the basis of its own priorities. Unlike the defunct business rate it is not a source of independent finance for local authorities. If a local authority area has a high percentage of businesses and firms within its boundaries, as all urban authorities do, then problems of traffic congestion ensue. To have the non-domestic rate under local control would be a useful source of transport funds.

Local authorities are required to produce a local transport plan (LTP) covering much of their proposed expenditure for the next five years. The plan has to be approved by central government. (See Box 2.2.)

Box 2.2 Local transport plans

Purposes

- Set transport in a wider context
- Set locally relevant targets for outcome indicators
- Identify the best value for money solutions to deliver those targets
- Set trajectories for key targets, to enable greater transparency and rigour in assessing performance

Priorities

- Reduce congestion
- Improve accessibility
- Safer roads
- Air quality

There is an inherent tension between central government vetting of local transport plans and local determination of what transport needs are. Because most of the funding for local transport comes from central government it is understandable that the centre wishes to ensure that its priorities are implemented by local authorities; yet local authorities will also have their own priorities and it has been a criticism of the process that local authorities cannot reflect these as much as they would like in the local transport plan.

This system of finance was introduced by the 1998 White Paper *A New Deal for Transport*, where there was also a strong emphasis on planning for local needs. In this White Paper there was the added proviso that there should be as much participation in the formulation of the LTP as possible from all those who could be construed as 'stakeholders'. This included local outposts of government agencies such as the Department for Employment, other departments of the local authority who had a legitimate interest in transport – education, social services and, in particular, the local NHS – alongside voluntary organizations such as those representing older people and people with disabilities, transport pressure groups and the representatives of local business. For many local authority transport departments this degree of participation was novel. There is a view that because local authority transport departments are staffed mainly by men with an engineering background then this kind of work was foreign to them. It is undeniable that for much of the post-war period local authority transport departments saw their role as building and maintaining the road system and that meeting 'transport need' was a secondary preoccupation.

The extent to which the LTP was a participative exercise taking account of the views of those opposed to the local authority's plans for the next five years is doubtful. The evidence shows that some local authorities made greater efforts than others to involve and engage stakeholders. Local transport plans need to be seen as part of the Labour government's commitment to partnership between stakeholders. This is a model of 'governance' meaning government at local, regional and national levels, acting in partnership with the private sector and with agencies in civil society. LTPs are a cornerstone of Labour's contribution to transport planning with this emphasis on partnership, stakeholders and the commitment to involve voluntary organizations. But the policy environment is a very different one from urban regeneration schemes or social services where these ideas are not so novel and so are more acceptable. Some local authorities employed firms of consultants for these participative exercises, so while they brought some expertise to the task it might be argued that the participation did not fully involve the local authority staff.

As well as transport responsibilities local authorities also have planning powers. Each local authority has to produce a local development framework (LDF) which must be set within regional spatial and transport policies. Unitary authorities have joint planning and transport powers. County councils have transport powers but not planning; planning powers are exercised by the district councils.

Decisions on land use are obviously very important for transport. In some parts of the country the demand for new housing development puts considerable pressure on the existing road network. The key document for the integration of transport and land-use planning is *Planning Policy Guidance 13: Transport* (Department of the Environment, Transport and the Regions 2001). This sets planning for transport within a sustainable development framework highlighting the importance of accessibility to services and facilities for those residents who do not have access to a car. The framework's other objectives are to reduce the need to travel 'especially by car' and the promotion of more sustainable travel choices for both people and freight (ibid.: 2–3).

Regional government

Each of the English regions has to produce a regional transport strategy to show how the government's transport strategy will be implemented and how a long-term transport strategy will be undertaken (Glaister et al. 2006: 150). The staff of the nine English regions are accountable to the regional assemblies which are not directly elected bodies but are composed mainly of councillors from the local authorities in the region. Also at the regional level are the government offices which work with the regional assembly and with local authorities in the implementation of government policy across ten policy areas, including transport. There is a clear steer in government advice on regional transport strategies that in planning for housing and economic development there needs to be an emphasis on public transport accessibility.

EU transport policy

The European Union's Directorate General for Transport and Energy formulates transport policy ideas and works to coordinate and integrate transport policy across the member states.

The EU has had an explicit transport policy since 1992 when it published its Common Transport Policy (European Commission 1992). Previous to this, transport had been recognized in the founding Treaty of Rome in 1957 as a significant policy area but there was always a tension between viewing it as an important part of economic activity and the desire of member states to retain control over their transport utilities. With the Maastricht treaty of 1991 and the creation of the single market, transport was seen as an area where liberalization could take place and over the past two decades this has been happening (Stevens 2004). Various restrictions have been removed: lorry firms can now transport goods in other countries and airlines can fly to other European countries.

Although in its official statements the EU is committed to 'sustainable mobility', over the past decade this has not necessarily meant that environmentally benign modes – walking and cycling – have prospered in member states. On the contrary, the number of cars is at an all-time high.

This is understandable given the commitment to economic development with increased transport movement being seen as an index of rising economic prosperity. The creation of an open economic market is seen as predicated upon an efficient transport system and this presupposes motorways and good road links. A great deal of money has been expended on the Trans-European Networks (TENs). The point of the TENs was to link up the transport infrastructure across the EU. TENs are not only road networks but also sea and rail routes. Since the accession countries of central and eastern Europe joined in 2004 there has been a commitment to building east–west routes to facilitate trade and commerce.

The EU's 2001 Transport White Paper proposed policies which would ensure a better balance between the modes, deal with congestion and reduce bottlenecks and road accidents (European Commission 2001). The authors were aware of the fact that mobility needs could easily be generated by decisions as to where factories, office and other places of employment were to be situated. Similarly there was a recognition that patterns of work and schooling are major determinants of travel behaviour so need to be taken into account in transport planning (Glaister et al. 2006).

The recent thrust of the European transport policy towards liberalization of markets is consistent with the direction taken by UK governments since the Conservatives came to power in 1979 so there have not been significant problems on this issue at least between Westminster and Brussels.

The mid-term review of the EU Transport White Paper, *Keep Europe Moving: Sustainable Mobility for our Continent* (European Commission 2006), reveals a deep-seated ambiguity in EU transport policy. This 'sustainable transport policy' has as its objectives the meeting of society's economic, social and environmental needs, the mobility of goods and people, and states that 'mobility is also an essential citizen right' (ibid.: 3). There is ample evidence here for those who might think that a 'sustainable mobility' policy is a contradiction in terms: the review tells us that one of the EU's transport objectives is to 'offer a high level of mobility to people and business throughout the Union', and goes on to state that another objective is 'to protect the environment'. This is a policy stance which commits the EU to a policy of supporting road building with direct subventions to many member states for them to build motorways and other major roads as it is believed that this will aid economic competitiveness. At the same time there is the belief that the environment can be protected despite the damage produced by major highways allowing lorries to transport goods the length and breadth of the continent. It must be said, however, that this is a policy stance shared by the great majority of the EU's 27 member states. It is an example of 'environmental modernization', namely the belief that economic growth can coexist with environmental protection and adjustment.

Some critics have argued that while the EU has been promoting sustainable *mobility* it has largely neglected the measures which would promote sustainable cities, that is to say cities where the energy requirements of transport would be considerably diminished because of the high percentage of citizens walking, cycling and using public transport. The moves towards sustainable transport would appear to have been subordinated to the imperatives of creating a free market in transport ensuring that the EU has been vigorous in its support of the liberalization of the aviation industry in the single European market.

Transport policy making

The straightforward answer to the question 'Who makes transport policy?' is government. But which government, for we now have sub-national government in Belfast, Cardiff and Edinburgh. The Department for Transport issues Transport White Papers, while local authorities have to work within the confines of current government policy as they are dependent on central government funding. Yet policy making at central, regional and local level takes place within a set of assumptions which determine the limits of policy decisions. The dominant policy assumption in transport planning for roads which went largely unchallenged until the 1990s was 'predict and provide'. In other words, transport planners came up with forecasts of the expected increase in the numbers of those who wanted to drive and would become drivers, and extrapolated from this the miles of new road space which would be required given the expected growth in traffic levels. This was a clear example of using transport policy to accommodate the growing numbers of cars on the roads and was heavily influenced by the pressure groups active on behalf of the motoring, petrol and road construction firms (Hamer 1987). Among these interest groups there was a belief that in the UK it was possible to build enough roads to cater for this increase in demand.

Box 2.3 UK transport policy time chart, 1998–2007

1998   White Paper *A New Deal for Transport*
2000   Transport Act
2000   Ten Year Plan
2002   London congestion charge
2004   White Paper *The Future of Transport*
2006   *The Eddington Transport Study*
2007   Stern Review, *The Economics of Climate Change*
2007   Discussion document *Towards a Sustainable Transport System*

Throughout the 1960s and 1970s this dominant form of transport planning resulted in traffic engineering solutions to problems of congestion and lack of capacity on the roads network. According to Grant (1977: 13), the process was characterized as:

1. identification of problems;
2. production of future environments;
3. the generation of alternative solutions;
4. the evaluation of solutions against a set of goals.

This was the period – the 1960s and 1970s – when large swathes of British cities were demolished in order to make space for urban trunk roads and motorways. In the second half of the twentieth century the belief that roads would boost the prosperity of a town, city or region was dominant. The look of many towns and cities was drastically changed in order to fulfil the perceived needs of the car. Motorway building started in the UK in the late 1950s; by 2006 there were 2,025 miles of motorway in England. Motorways were often behind this transformation of the urban landscape for many cities wanted the new motorways to reach into their heart.

Grant distinguished between two groups of transport planners: those who held to 'predict and provide' in the post-war period he labelled 'traditionalists', while the non-traditionalists were those who pointed out that the assumptions of a 'car-owning democracy' were far from the reality of many people's lives as they did not own cars or have access to a car. Among these could be numbered the poor, the old, many men and women and all children (Grant 1977: 14).

'Predict and provide' was an extraordinarily powerful policy paradigm with an apparent link to the future. Those who argued from this position seemingly had understood the shape of the future and road building was all of a piece with progress, economic development and increased prosperity. Vigar drawing on the work of Hajer (Hajer 1995) identifies 'predict and provide' as a policy discourse which framed the reality of transport planning: 'It is variably made up of a number of storylines (such as "roads for prosperity") and practices (such as forecasting techniques and modelling procedures)' (Vigar 2002: 17).

Although both Labour and Conservative parties were committed to the extension of car ownership, the Labour Party was keener on promoting public transport in urban areas. In the 1960s and 1970s the railways were still a nationalized industry and bus services were either local authority controlled and run or part of the National Bus Company so central government had much more ability to influence their policy direction.

The high point of post-war 'predict and provide' thinking was undoubtedly the Conservative government's *Roads for Prosperity* White Paper of 1989. This was based on projections of an increase in traffic on Britain's roads of between 83 per cent and 142 per cent by 2020. The government announced an unprecedented programme of road building – the biggest since the Romans according to the then Secretary of State for Transport, Paul Channon. Almost immediately the new road plans were announced they ran into concerted opposition at a number of sites around the country.

The decision to put the M3 through the beautiful countryside at Twyford Down, near Winchester, was one such where an alliance of environmentalists, local people and national pressure groups assembled and fought a long battle against the road's construction. The decision was made to go ahead with the road despite the fact that it would destroy a Site of Special Scientific Interest, two Scheduled Ancient Monuments and an Area of Outstanding Natural Beauty. The Newbury by-pass was another where twelve archaeological sites, nature reserves, an Area of Outstanding Natural Beauty and three Sites of Special Scientific Interest were lost. But here again there were contradictory pressures, for the Conservative government had signed up to sustainable development as a policy aim in 1992 at the Rio Earth Summit and there were those in the government who felt there was a contradiction between this commitment and more road building. In the event, the Conservative government trimmed back its road building plans and announced in 1996 that several schemes would not now go ahead. Sixty-nine road schemes were suspended, 49 others were scrapped and 173 were delayed (Vigar 2002: 75). The alliances which developed between rural residents who objected to new roads scarring the countryside and the green activists who were prepared to use direct action and sometimes risk their lives to stop the bulldozers may well have been a significant consideration for a government which did not want to lose seats in rural constituencies because of the roads issue.

The beginning of the 1990s saw the emergence of an alternative vision of the transport future. This was 'the new realism' propounded by Phil Goodwin (Goodwin et al. 1991), who argued that the UK could not build itself out of the congestion on the roads as more roads generate more traffic. What had to occur was not wholesale road building but instead a judicious programme of road improvements within a new context of demand management, that is to say, encouraging car drivers to use other modes such as walking, cycling or public transport. The encouragement would involve not merely exhortation or public education campaigns but also parking restrictions in congested areas together with charging for roads. Unless this was attempted the congestion on the roads would worsen, damaging the quality of life for everyone.

In opposition in the 1990s the Labour Party adopted many of these new realist ideas: John Prescott MP contributed the foreword to a collection of essays on sustainable transport when he was shadow transport minister in 1992 (Roberts et al. 1992). In power, his super-ministry the Department of the Environment, Transport and the Regions produced *A New Deal for Transport* (1998) which was a radical break with previous transport thinking and policy, outlining the ways in which public transport, walking and cycling would be promoted and car use discouraged. Upon taking office he had famously declared: 'I will have failed if in five years' time there are not many more people using public transport and far fewer journeys by car'

(Shaw and Docherty 2008: 9–10). His failure to deliver owed much to the coalition of support that Labour had assembled in order to win the election of 1997. Labour had succeeded in detaching 'Middle England' from its tradition of voting Conservative but had done so by trying hard not to frighten the aspirational middle class. The prime minister, Tony Blair, was concerned that some of the measures contained in *A New Deal for Transport* would lead to the government being labelled in the media as 'anti-motorist'. There were other considerations. It was rumoured that Tesco did not appreciate the idea of taxing parking spaces in out-of-town retail parks, especially when the company was being canvassed to give financial support to the Millennium Dome and, whether this was the case or not, the proposal did not make it into the White Paper. The Transport Act 2000, which was the legislative embodiment of *A New Deal for Transport*, was a timid affair. It gave powers to introduce road user charging but there was to be no national scheme; instead local authorities were given the power to charge road users. Unsurprisingly, few were interested, as if adopted by one local authority but not by the surrounding authorities then it would deter shoppers and possibly in the longer term would be hindrance to attracting firms.

Ken Livingstone, then mayor of London, used the powers in the 2000 Act and, showing great political leadership, in 2003 implemented the London congestion charge in spite of substantial opposition and no support from the Labour government. Four years later, overall traffic levels were down 15 per cent. Car, van and lorry traffic was 30 per cent lower and congestion levels had fallen by 20 per cent (Eddington 2006: 165).

The fuel protests of 2000 combined with the wish of the government not to appear 'anti-motorist' resulted in a transport policy which was not anti any mode but pro them all and has resulted in the exacerbation of the problems which Labour faced when it came to power in 1997. Now with 6 million more vehicles on the roads than in 1997 it has continued with the policy of increasing road space: the road network has grown by 258 route kilometres in the decade 1996–2006 which is equivalent to 8 per cent (Parkhurst and Dudley 2008: 57).

Protest and pressure groups

Transport became a contested political arena in the 1960s when in urban areas councils began to push through plans for major road schemes. Community action groups sprang up to protect their areas. These were joined in the 1970s by environmental groups – the best known being Friends of the Earth – alarmed at the environmental destruction which road building created. Today there are a range of environmental transport groups such as the Campaign for Better Transport (formerly Transport 2000), Living Streets (formerly the Pedestrians Association) and Sustrans. These are cause groups based on individual membership but for some of their work they are now funded by government and the National Lottery. The best known example of this is the National Cycle Network which was funded by and established by Sustrans. Living Streets – the campaign for walking – benefits from Department of Health funding in its drive to get more people physically active.

The influence of these groups is diffuse. Some have a network of local branches which exercise influence to varying degrees on local authorities promoting a sustainable transport agenda.

There are other environmental organizations which do not have transport as their primary purpose but from time to time will be active participants in transport issues. These include the Campaign to Protect Rural England (CPRE), the Royal Society for the Protection of Birds (RSPB) and the Civic Trust. Then there are single-issue groups which spring up in response to a particular development: it might be a proposed new road, or a campaign against airport expansion.

Clearly the degree of influence on the policy-making process which these groups possess is related to a host of factors: their representativeness, the size of their membership and the regard in which they are held by important political actors. Financial resources are clearly important, for well funded groups can commission research, employ press officers, liaise with government departments.

Those who want to keep the dominant role which the car has assumed in our society have been among the most successful of the interest groups in recent political history. One of Britain's biggest pressure groups, the Automobile Association (AA) – membership over 15 million – together with the RAC – membership of 6 million – regularly campaign on behalf of what they see as the interest of the motorist (Glaister et al. 2006: 177). Of course, these very large membership figures are a result of the breakdown services offered by the two organizations rather than a desire to help promote the interests of motorists. Motor manufacturers themselves are also keen to influence government decisions and are vigilant in promoting their interests. The decline in the number of jobs in motor manufacturing as British firms lost out to foreign competition and were either liquidated or taken over by their foreign competitors has meant that the 'national interest' argument is much less important now than it once was. Nevertheless those employed in motor manufacture still represent a sizeable chunk, around 6.5 per cent, of the total UK manufacturing workforce.

Some drivers believe that the AA and the RAC do not properly represent the views of motorists. One such body is the Association of British Drivers, which campaigns vigorously against speed cameras, reduced speed limits and other measures which it feels impinge upon the freedom of motorists. While this may be a small organization in terms of membership there can be no doubt that it represents a definite strand of opinion which is opposed to road user charging for example. An indication of how strong feeling was on road user charging was displayed in early 2007 when over 1.8 million people signed a petition on the No. 10 Downing Street website against the idea.

Among the more powerful groups in the transport lobby can be counted those that represent business interests: the Society of Motor Manufacturers and Traders, the Freight Transport Association, the Road Haulage Association and the Association of Train Operating Companies. They have their counterpart in the trade unions with the Transport and General Workers Union, the Associated Society of Locomotive Engineers and Firemen (ASLEF), and the Rail and Maritime Transport Union.

Conclusion

The 1960s saw a change in the political salience of transport in the UK. The post-war rebuilding of British cities led to proposals for major road schemes which would accommodate the increase in the number of road vehicles. Government was of the view that good transport links were vital to a prosperous economy. But not everyone agreed: many of the people who were to lose their homes because of new roads could be counted among them, and, as we have seen, there was a gradual and growing concern from the environmental lobby. Over the past forty years road building has led to successive battles, be they direct action – people actually sitting down in front of bulldozers to prevent construction – or public inquiries, which were often long drawn-out battles between protestors and the Highways Agency.

At first the opposition to road building came primarily from those who were going to be affected by a new scheme. From the 1970s onwards though, they had new allies with the emergence of environmental pressure groups, principally Friends of the Earth and Greenpeace. Gradually the opposition to new roads for more cars has become an environmental cause and more recently a social issue as the impact of a car-based society on social relationships and community has become more apparent.

It is salutary to remember that the planning horizon of many transport projects is long, much longer than the five-year focus of politicians fixated on the next election. Understandably, politicians are nervous about alienating public opinion which, as the fuel protests of 2000 show, can quickly turn against a government. If we are to be kind to Labour we can say that the failure to move towards the sustainable transport goals of *A New Deal for Transport* are not only a failure of political leadership but also a failure of the UK's political and policy-making system.

This does not bode well for the social and environmental challenges which the country faces and which are outlined in subsequent chapters.

Further reading

Glaister, S., Burnham, J., Stevens, H. and Travers, T. (2006). *Transport Policy in Britain*, 2nd edn. Basingstoke: Palgrave Macmillan. An excellent guide to the dimensions of transport policy.

Docherty, I. and Shaw, J. (eds) (2008). *Traffic Jam: Ten Years of 'Sustainable' Transport in the UK*. Bristol: Policy Press. A critical account of Labour's transport policy by a range of academics.

From public to private transport

Always the towns have remained fundamentally the same in character, for they have existed to serve the little-changing needs of generation after generation of little-changing people. But now, suddenly as it were, a startling new habit has developed. A single invention, in the course of a few years' development, has placed within the grasp of every man and woman a means of rapid *personal* movement ten to twenty times faster than walking. It is not a matter of building a few new roads, it is a matter of dealing with a new social situation. New urban arrangements are needed if the killing and the wounding, the noise and stink and confusion are to be avoided. Alternatively, the old arrangements may yet suffice if the new mobility is surrendered, or at least drastically restrained. It is certain that there has never been a choice so significant to the future of our towns.

(Buchanan 1958: 207)

In the twentieth century there occurred a major change in the way that people travelled, a movement from public transport – railways and buses – to the car. This chapter describes that transition and then examines the ways in which the car has transformed society and individuals' sense of themselves. The car, powered by fossil fuels, is central to the debate on the future of transport, environment and society. The shift from public to private has had a profound impact on human relationships, localities and society, but of course the public – public transport, public space – has not disappeared and towns and cities have had to negotiate a new modus vivendi between public transport and public space on the one hand and private transport on the other. Another way of thinking about motorization is in terms of mobility, the car bestows on drivers the ability to travel whenever and seemingly wherever they choose. Along with this goes the powerful notion of freedom, as the car frees the motorist from the constraints of timetables and fixed routes. Yet this freedom and flexibility come at a price which the twenty-first century will have to pay with the impact of global warming. The growing evidence on the contribution of carbon emissions to climate change has stimulated much work on the alternatives to the petrol-powered car and the chapter concludes with a consideration of their feasibility.

Public transport

In the wake of the industrial revolution the social consequences of the transport infrastructure in this country have been profound. The economy and culture of towns and cities were radically changed by the arrival of the railway. The fact that from the 1840s it was possible to read the London morning papers in northern cities on the day they were published helped to contribute towards making Britain a national society. The early nineteenth-century fishing village of Brighton became a premier seaside resort because of the very large numbers of people who could, from the 1840s, travel down by train to Brighton from London for a day trip. Aside from leisure, the introduction of workmen's trains – trains with lower fares to enable people to get to work – meant that working people as well as the middle class could live further from their place of employment. Much of the development of south London was determined by the extension of the railway line from central London (Wolmar 2007).

In addition to the expansion of the railways, public transport became an important force in the late nineteenth century with the emergence of electric trams, later replaced by buses in the early twentieth century. Trains, trams and buses allowed the middle and working classes to live at greater distances from their place of work. If the forms of transport in a society reflect the organization and ethos of that society they also help to determine it. Nineteenth-century society was highly stratified, but all classes used the railway. This meant that there was a clear class system in the organization of the railway, with first class (comfortable seats and furnishings), second class (upholstered seats) and third class (wooden seats). Porters and station staff were known as 'railway servants' and there were a great many of them, for railways were extremely labour intensive. The railway reflected the highly stratified society that was ruled over by Queen Victoria.

It would be misleading to characterize the major transport trend as being solely the shift from public transport to the car because the bicycle was another means of personal transport which had a great impact from the late nineteenth century through to the middle of the twentieth century. For working-class men in the period between the two world wars cycling was an important form of transport. Cycling became a popular leisure activity for both sexes before the First World War, while bikes also became a favoured form of transport for working-class men for the journey to and from work. The bicycle was a form of personal transport for commuting journeys for many people before the advent of the car.

The arrival of mass motoring and mass mobility meant much greater freedom to travel when and where one wanted, but the negative consequences of this 'greater mobility for some' were generally ignored, as were the costs for the environment and society. For those with access to a car, flexibility and freedom had been introduced into their lives: this was extolled not just by motor manufacturers and the motoring organizations but also by government in its transport policy. In contrast, for non-car-owning people and households there were a great many losses as the public transport network declined year on year, and cyclists and walkers found their journeys made more difficult by increasing traffic. The reduction in public transport use stems from the fact that once a person bought a car then he or she would be much less likely to use public transport. Figure 3.1 demonstrates the take-off in motor car ownership and the corresponding decrease in the number of people using buses and trains.

The consequence for those non-drivers who relied on public transport was a gradual decline in bus and rail services, and with passenger numbers dropping there was less revenue to sustain services so cuts began to be made. This was seen most vividly on the railways where the Conservative government of Harold Macmillan, which built Britain's first motorway in 1959,

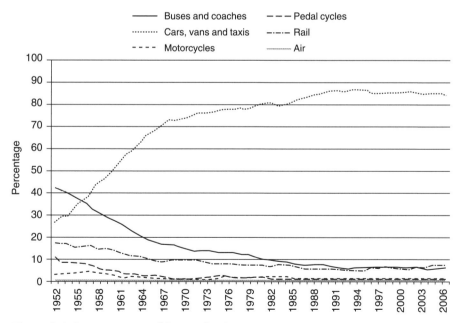

Figure 3.1 Passenger travel by mode, Great Britain, 1952–2006

Source: Department for Transport 2008c: table 1.1

commissioned Dr Beeching to review the rail network in order to make it more efficient. In his report published in 1963 Beeching recommended the wholesale closure of many branch lines and much of this programme was carried through in the 1960s.

For the past half century, public transport has been seen as a poor alternative to the car and the road network. Successive governments have referred to 'investment' in new roads whereas money for public transport is a 'subsidy'.

The motorization of society has meant that many services and facilities have been decentralized: food shops, places of employment, hospitals, schools and colleges. Depending on where you live, much of the basic infrastructure of contemporary society – shopping centres, sports centres and hospitals – is difficult to reach if you do not have a car. Similarly, in the twentieth century, the road network meant there was a marked redistribution of population, with the prospect of living in the countryside and working in the city a real option for many people given fast roads and cars. The 'compact city', built around public transport with a central business district and radial spokes leading out to suburbs, is no more. New urban areas with offices, industry and housing are likely to be decentralized, reflecting car dependence. Buses gradually began to replace trams in British cities from the beginning of the twentieth century. Buses were cheaper than trains, providing a more flexible service. Their problem once mass car ownership came about was twofold: loss of revenue and traffic congestion which meant that they had a much harder job trying to keep to the timetable.

In Figure 3.1 we see that cars, which started from a low position in 1952, have outstripped all other transport modes in terms of passenger kilometres travelled.

There has been a significant decline in bus travel. The number of local bus passenger journeys in England fell from over 16 billion in 1950 to 4 billion in 1999/2000 although there has been a small increase subsequently to 4.5 billion (Commission for Integrated Transport 2004: 9; Department for Transport 2009c: 21).

Over the past half century the image of the bus suffered to the point where many people believed that it was only a transport option for those who could not afford to own a car. In major urban areas this is less the case and least so in London where bus use has increased 75 per cent since 1985/86 (Department for Transport 2009c: 35).

If we look at households with cars and the number of cars in each household then we can see from Figure 3.2 that in 1980 41 per cent of households did not have a car whereas by 2006 this figure had declined to 24 per cent. This means that there are now more households with access to two cars (26 per cent) than there are with access to no car (Department for Transport 2009c: 21).

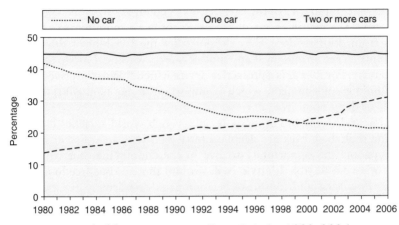

Figure 3.2 Household access to a car, Great Britain, 1980–2006

Source: Department for Transport 2009c: 21

The power of the car

From its beginnings in the motor workshops of Germany in the 1880s the car has gone on to become a revolutionary and ubiquitous technology. In the twentieth century 1 billion cars were built. There are now over 750 million cars on the world's roads. In the UK in the first half of the twentieth century, cars and other modes of transport coexisted, but in the second half of the century there was a radical shift, with cars becoming the dominant means of mobility. The emergence of the car as a mass market good coincided with the emergence of mass consumer societies in the rich world. The car has a central role in consumer society. It is the consumer good *par excellence* in that it is not just a machine for getting from A to B but is also a reflection of one's status, one's sexuality, one's orientation in the world.

No one needs to be told about the numerous different models of cars and the ways in which they are advertised in order to create a particular elite or mass appeal. In keeping with the temper of our times there is a belief that one's identity is reflected in the car that one drives. Because cars are 'personal' transport, as opposed to the public transport of trains and buses, they can be said to reflect one's personality and are for each individual one of the principal ways of viewing the world. Although the car is exactly the same as the next one produced by that manufacturer, the motorist is encouraged to think that, with modifications – a particular CD player or air-conditioning system for example – they can personalize the vehicle.

As consumerism goes global, persuading more and more people that shopping is a central purpose in life, we see newly emerging consumer societies such as China and India promoting the car at the expense of the bicycle. The popularity of the car is easily accounted for by its convenience: apart from the bicycle, none of the other forms of mobility take the occupants from door to door, they do not offer the freedom of the car, with the ability to get up and go at any time of one's choosing. Nor do they afford the security. For the car is a protective device which shields the driver from the surrounding environment, which is important if one is moving through a hostile or dangerous area.

So integral to the life of many people in rich-world societies has the car become that their lives are deeply intertwined with it – the car has given many people the opportunity to live in the countryside but work in the city, to have a flexible lifestyle built around the car. But freedom like this has its downside and motorists become car dependent to the extent that many cannot live without their vehicle. Their way of life becomes something which only the car can provide. Many people have to have a car to get to work – there is no public transport which will perform this journey. Car dependence is a recognized condition in modern life. It has its personal aspects as well, for many people invest emotionally in their car – they might give it a name – and enjoy the feelings they get from this material object. They depend on it as they might another close human being. These emotions might include the feeling of exhilaration they get when travelling at speed or the feelings of protection and security they derive from the car. They are what Mimi Sheller has termed 'automotive emotions': 'feelings, passions and embodied experiences' associated with driving (Sheller 2003). Driving is a technical skill, the acquisition of which is seen by many as an important transport milestone in their life, having the same status as, say, learning to walk. Countries vary in the age at which they permit people to drive, but generally it is between the ages of 17 and 21. It is also close to the age when young people achieve adult status, and for many it is viewed as part of becoming an adult. A similar age to when young people are allowed to vote, but one may suspect that the right to drive is often valued more highly than the right to vote. (A small survey of young people in London a few years ago bore this out (Solomon 1998).)

The hegemony of cars in transport policy and society has had innumerable consequences. The freedom which the car gives to the individual motorist has led to an opening up of the possibilities for many people regarding where they live, where they work, where they travel, leading to a great deal of enjoyment and satisfaction. But at the macro level the individual decisions which are made every day – where to live and how to travel – have resulted in a decentralization of housing and work and other facilities such as shops and leisure. One of the consequences of this is that people are travelling further to get to work and to reach the shops. At the beginning of the 1970s people travelled about 4,500 miles a year on average whereas today it is around 7,100 miles a year (Metz 2008: 5).

The freedoms bestowed on motorists by the car can only be provided by the car. Other forms of transport do not provide its individual mobility. This means that it is difficult once people become motorists for them to consider using other forms of transport. Hence the difficulties in contemporary UK transport policy in trying to achieve 'modal shift', i.e. using a bike or a bus instead of the car – using another mode. As the car is a significant financial investment, second only to buying a house, then, understandably, if it is standing outside one's front door, why leave it there, go to the bus stop and pay a bus fare?

The emergence of the car

From its first appearance on the roads the car has been a status symbol – at first the preserve of the rich but later, with the creation of the Model T Ford, a 'people's car' emerged in the USA. The Ford began to demonstrate the ways in which the economy and society would change – farmers found they could get their produce to market quicker and people in outlying areas in the countryside were connected for the first time to the cities. The people's car concept was further developed with the Volkswagen inspired by Adolf Hitler in 1930s Germany.

But the car was not universally loved and it took some decades for it to win over public opinion. In the early years of motoring, the 1890s and the period before the First World War, the dust that cars created on the untarmacked roads made them unpopular with other road users. As their engines improved and speeds increased, road 'accidents' became a new source of danger. In August 1896 Bridget Driscoll, who was crossing the road in south London, became the first road death after she was hit by a passing car (Pugh 2008: 239). Now there are approximately eight people killed on the roads every day in the UK. One has to remember that roads and streets were much more inclusive places when the car first emerged. People walked, cycled, used buses and trams . . . and year by year there were more deaths and serious injuries. By the 1920s road deaths had rocketed, along with serious injuries. 'Taking the inter-war period as a whole the total casualties included 120,000 fatalities and 1.5 million injuries, making motoring comparable to fighting a war' (Pugh 2008: 246). The lesson was being learnt that the road was now the preserve of the car and the pavements became the refuge of the pedestrian. Road deaths in the 1920s were higher than they are today although there were many fewer cars on the roads. The state moved slowly to protect the population and in the face of this carnage pedestrian crossings, speed limits and the driving test were all introduced, despite the opposition of the Automobile Association.

Before the First World War the car was the preserve of the upper class, who more often than not would employ a chauffeur rather than drive the vehicle themselves. It was in the inter-war period that the middle classes discovered the delights of motoring, many of them moving from a stance of hostility to the car to enthusiasm for the freedoms it bestowed upon them. Sean O'Connell notes in his history of the car that once car ownership spread to the middle class then there was little chance that an 'effective opposition to private motoring' would arise (O'Connell 1998: 143). Typical was the writer Virginia Woolf and her husband Leonard who, upon the purchase of their first car, could write: 'Nothing ever changed so profoundly my material existence . . . as the possession of a motor car' (quoted in Thacker in Böhm et al. 2006: 180). A sentiment echoed by millions of new motorists since then. Thacker notes that the middle-class motorists of the 1920s and 1930s used their new freedom to explore the countryside and, specifically, sites of historical interest. One might add that this trend was to grow in the post-war period as the National Trust took over more and more country houses and stately homes where it was almost essential to have a car to visit them.

In the Second World War, with petrol rationing, the number of cars on the roads declined dramatically. In 1939 on the outbreak of war there were 2 million cars on the roads, but this fell to 700,000 by 1943 (Plowden 1971: 311). The post-war age of mass motoring could not of course have been predicted, so that in the 1940s with petrol rationing still in place those who were planning the post-war cities and towns had little awareness that mass car ownership would mean that council tenants would want to drive cars just as much as white-collar workers (Sherlock 1991). The end of petrol rationing in the early 1950s enabled the creation of the mass car market, an important part of 'the affluent society'.

Conceptualizing the car

For most of the twentieth century the revolutionary technology of the car which was transforming society, space and our sense of time was ignored by sociologists. Why this should have been the case is not clear. Perhaps part of the answer lies in the fact that the car became such an all-pervasive feature of our society. It was not cars as such but car workers who became the object of study, with the 'affluent worker' studies which examined whether their material prosperity as part of the skilled working class had changed their political and social attitudes (Goldthorpe et al. 1968). The car workers of Luton and Dagenham were seen as an important barometer of social change.

In the community studies literature of post-war British empirical sociology the impact of the car rarely enters the discussion. Community studies as a sociological area begin in the 1950s when the motor car was about to change working-class areas as it became increasingly affordable. There is no discussion of the car at all in *Coal is Our Life*, a study of a local mining community 'Ashton' on the borders of the West Yorkshire and South

Yorkshire coalfields by Norman Dennis, Cliff Slaughter and Fernando Henriques. The authors merely record that 'Ashton is within easy reach of three substantial towns, and there are frequent bus services to each' (Dennis et al. 1956: 15). This is understandable given that Ashton was a mining town, with the great majority of men employed in the pits, and the study was done in the early 1950s. However, in her study of Banbury, a more mixed social class locale, carried out in the period 1948–51, Margaret Stacey only mentions transport as an occupational category (Stacey 1960). (One should add that there is, unsurprisingly, some discussion of cars in the Banbury re-study conducted in the late 1960s (Stacey et al. 1975).)

Although the work of Peter Willmott and Michael Young at the Institute of Community Studies in the 1950s was concerned with analysing the movement of large numbers of people out of London to greenfield locations at some distance from their relations, work and leisure, the transport impli-cations of this were not a major consideration for the authors. Whether this was the case for their respondents we do not know. In their book *Family and Kinship in East London* they compare the lives of Bethnal Green residents with those families who have moved out of London to 'Greenleigh' (Debden in Essex). Young and Willmott point to the problems faced by those who live on the estate in reaching work, schools and shops if they do not have a car. They quote one local resident who told them: 'there are two things that I think are essential when you live on an estate. One's a telephone, the other's a car' (Young and Willmott 1957: 131).

The economic and social forces which determine employment opportun-ities for people in a locality are nowadays national and increasingly global. This obviously changes the nature of the local community and hence of community studies. Access to work and contact with relations in the extended family are facilitated and often only made possible because of the car. It does not mean, however, that what happens in the locality is not of concern to residents. There is an issue of the degree of interconnectedness or connectivity of people. Those with a high degree of connectedness – to friends, family at a distance, neighbours – will more often than not be well connected with the new technologies of communication: the Internet, mobile phones. To them the locality matters less than to those who do not have the opportunity to drive.

Mobilities

Contemporary sociology has tried to theorize the car-dependent societies within which we live. It has done this using the idea of mobilities which, as a term, enables the discussion of information and communication technology, migration and tourism as well as car driving and other modes of transport.

The answer which John Urry and the proponents of mobilities would give to the question we posed earlier as to why British sociology ignored the car, would presumably be that it was a 'sedentarist' sociology, meaning that it 'locates bounded and authentic places as the fundamental basis of human experience' (Urry 2007: 31). Urry argues that society has become a redundant concept given the globalizing forces and technologies which have transformed space, time and distance (Urry 2000). This is a helpful perspective because it enables us to see the car as part of a network of mobilities which are changing the way we work and play because of their interconnectivity. For example, many people can accomplish office tasks in their (parked) cars via mobile phones and personal digital assistants which means they do not need to rely on an office base. Urry argues that time and space have been automobilized. They are now experienced and seen through the means of cars which enable people to juggle with time and space. But the mobilities paradigm in sociology goes much further than theorizing the relationship between modes of transport and society because it aims to theorize the social world 'as a wide array of economic, social and political practices, infrastructures and ideologies that all involve, entail or curtail various kinds of movement of people, or ideas, or information or objects' (Urry 2007: 18).

The concept of automobility is central. It has two meanings, one being self propelled mobility, as with cycling or walking, and the second the structures, institutions and policies which underpin and facilitate car driving. In the words of Bohm et al. (2006: 3): 'a set of political institutions and practices that seek to organise, accelerate and shape the spatial movements and impacts of automobilites, while simultaneously regulating their many consequences'.

Bohm et al. argue that automobility is also an ideology in which notions such as freedom, privacy, progress and autonomy are centred on the car. This is persuasive because there are so many examples of freedom being associated with cars. The teenager who learns to drive experiences a freedom; he or she does not have to rely on lifts from parents. It is the 'freedom to break loose and drive off' (Böhm et al. 2006: 122). Freedom has been invoked by motorist organizations when campaigning against what they perceive as restrictions on their liberty such as seat belts, safety cameras and speed limits. We talk about 'the private motorist' and this reinforces the association of the car with privacy. It is as though, for some motorists, they are invisible in their cars and are 'free' to do what they like. It is a private space and many people value this privacy after their working day. The car is also a vehicle which promotes privacy in society as thousands of cars make their ways through cities with the people inside them seeing the world and other people but not having to acknowledge them. One of the consequences for our streets, roads, avenues, drives is that they are deprived of people walking along, so again enhancing privacy.

Progress is another notion connected with the car; it is certainly associated with the construction of highways and motorways. The developing world is being transformed by the creation of super-highways such as the Asia Europe highway, and the EU has regarded the construction of major roads and motorways in peripheral regions of Europe as a central part of its transport policy. In the past twenty years Spain, Portugal and Ireland have been among the countries which have had European money given to them to build these roads. On a smaller scale it is regarded as progress if roads are constructed which link villages to towns and cities, as is being done in the developing world with the aid of funds from the World Bank and other investment banks. Autonomy is, as we have already noted, central to our relationship with the car. In so many areas of social life, if a person does not have a car then life can be more difficult and there will be many activities in which they will not be able to participate. Contemporary society is organized on the assumption that we are independent actors, that we are autonomous, and the car is the technology which enables this – it is not the only one for there are others such as mobile phones and computers. Autonomy in working practices has meant that for many people they do not have a workplace but can work in their company car where, with a hand-held device, they are able to use the Internet and the phone network independent of a fixed location.

Automobility is a way of experiencing the world, producing the 'automotive emotions' which Mimi Sheller has discussed. Apart from the fact that motorists experience various emotions in relation to their cars it is useful to remember that they experience the world through a glass screen: they are on the inside looking out, feeling safe within their private space but aware of the dangerousness of the wider world (Jain and Guiver 2001).

The category of motorist also demands some attention. For many people, being a motorist is no more a description of themselves than 'human being'. The motorists organizations, the AA and the RAC, can claim to speak on behalf of motorists yet their membership of millions have joined mainly in order to get the support of the breakdown service, not because they want to belong to a campaigning organization for motorists. At certain points and in certain contexts, 'motorist' is a role which gives people a commonality one with another. In a variety of social contexts, conversations are often about the traffic or the journey that one has just undertaken. These are conversations which people can only have because of their relationship with a machine – the car gives them the entrée into these conversations which they would not have if they had caught the bus. But we are also dealing with what Urry calls 'hybrids' of machines and people where the car driver relies on machines and the infrastructure of roads to help guide the driver. The car driver is a combination of human being and the technology of the car together with the system of signs, roads, petrol stations, which constitute the urban environment. Tim Dant agrees that there is a process of interpenetration between the car and the driver: 'an extension of the human body and an extension of technology and society into the human' (Dant 2004: 75).

As Dant points out, driving a car is not just using one mode among many transport modes, it is a way of experiencing and visualizing the world at speed under one's own control which it is difficult to see disappearing even in a post-carbon world.

'Motorist' is not a category which is utilized in many relevant contexts. For example, we know that the problem of physical inactivity in contemporary society is caused in some part by the over-reliance by some people on their cars and the consequent lack of walking. Yet discussions of obesity, heart disease and other conditions exacerbated by lack of physical activity are not related to the status of motorist. Discussions in the media do not talk about the obesity rates among motorists or the level of type 2 diabetes among motorists (Freund and Martin 2004). Perhaps this neglect of motorist as an identity is illustrative of the pervasiveness of car culture. It is not a discussion which some powerful interests would want to occur and it has become part of the common sense of our age that we are all motorists.

To be a motorist is to be a person with some power, not just horse power, but the power to make things happen. It means that this personal power is given some importance and this can be seen in gender relations with women aspiring to have an equality with men not just in the workplace but in ownership of a car. The 'family' car of the 1950s reflected the male breadwinner view of the world with the man taking the car to work leaving his stay-at-home wife to cope with the demands of shopping and looking after the children without the benefit of a vehicle. Since the emergence of the first car on to the road, being a motorist has been associated with masculinity. As O'Connell has observed about the middle-class motorists of the inter-war period: 'for the middle class male engaged in professional or commercial activity the model of car he drove made a statement about his success in the masculine world of work' (O'Connell 1998: 64). Obtaining a driving licence has become a rite of passage for a young man: 'So much so, that it is possible to claim that "the greatest shame for a grown man is to admit that he cannot drive a car" ' (*Sunday Times Magazine* 18 February 1990 cited in O'Connell 1998: 221). The ideology of feminism has been used by car manufacturers to suggest that car ownership is a way of increasing a woman's power and autonomy.

Is the power of the motorist one which derives from the power of the machine itself? Dant (2004) argues that we should think of the car driver as an entity, a fusion of person and machine.

Carless or car free?

To be carless – not driving a car and not having access to a car – in a car-dependent society can be viewed as a disability, for non-drivers are unable to perform a range of tasks which are open to motorists. This will vary from place to place, country to country, and is dependent on the rate of motorization. If a non-driver lives in the centre of most cities in the UK then it is not such a problem until he or she wants to leave the city and travel to another part of the country. Living in a country in which the majority of the population do not use a car there will be public transport and extensive use of cycling and walking. But to be carless or car free, depending on how one looks at it, in a highly motorized society is difficult. If you live in Venice it is not a problem, but it is a problem if you live in Los Angeles. There are some small initiatives in the UK which support the choice to go car free. Car clubs are springing up in which the members pay an annual fee to share a car (Sloman 2006). Similarly, we are seeing the small beginnings of car-free housing where residents sign an agreement not to own a car and no parking spaces are provided.

Privatization of lifestyles

The car has been associated with the decline of chance encounters gained walking along the street or meeting someone on the bus. It is a technology which permits motorists to do more than non-motorists, to accomplish more tasks as in the 'chained' journey where as well as, say, picking up the children from school the motorist parent can collect the dry cleaning and something for tea. But the technology of the car also encourages motorists to do more which can add to their stress. It is a machine which insulates the driver from the rest of the world (Jain and Guiver 2001), and it nowadays forms a crucial part of the nexus of the mobile individual. It can readily be seen that because the car is a personal(ized) form of transport it belongs to people in a way that is not possible with public transport. This can lead to a possessiveness which results occasionally in the phenomenon of 'road rage'.

   As a technology, cars have been very influential in the ways in which they have moulded and shaped society and social arrangements. Robert Putnam's book *Bowling Alone* – the discussion of social capital and its decline in the USA – puts much of the blame for this on the television, but he might equally well have attributed some of the responsibility to the automobile (Putnam 2000). In neighbourhoods where there is a high degree of car ownership the opportunities to meet one's neighbours by chance in the street are reduced because so few people walk. In order to accommodate this car-based way of life housing has to be spread out and so densities are quite low. This then means that there is not the available population to sustain a bus service or indeed other facilities. This process has progressed much further in the USA than in the UK but has been occurring here, creating many out-of-town housing estates where it is essential to have access to a car.

Cars and the city

The hegemony of the car means that cities and towns have been transformed in order to accommodate them. Large amounts of land have been required for car parking both in public car parks and at places of work. Extensive areas are given over to car-related activities: garages, service stations, motorway service areas, and all the associated car industries.

The architect Richard Rogers is clear: 'it is the car which has played the critical role in undermining the cohesive social structure of the city' (Rogers 1997: 35). There can be no doubt that planning for the car in the modern city is one of the most intractable problems which faces local government. In the period since Sir Colin Buchanan issued his report *Traffic in Towns*, which highlighted the problems posed to the structure and environment of cities by continuing car growth, cities have, in the main, attempted to accommodate the car (Buchanan 1963). But the costs of doing so are high and are often borne by those who have least resources, people living on low incomes without access to a car. Donald Appleyard showed the effect of heavy traffic on social relationships in San Francisco, namely that there was far less social interaction and contact among neighbours on the heavily trafficked street as opposed to those with lower traffic levels (Appleyard 1982). In 2008, Joshua Hart was able to show that a similar process occurred in Bristol. In a study of three streets in Bristol: 'Light Street' which had 140 vehicles a day passing through it, 'Medium Street' which had 8,420 vehicles and 'Heavy Street' which had 21,130 vehicles passing along it. As might be expected, people living on Heavy Street knew far fewer of their neighbours than those on the other two streets and their view as to the extent of their home territory was far more constricted than on the other streets. Hart concludes: 'All in all, Light Street is a community where people were relatively content with the local environment and their neighbours – a street with a healthy social life, a lower incidence of stress than the other two streets, a support network that they could rely on during rough times, for example when they became ill, or after the death of a spouse' (Hart 2008: 33). Such evidence shows that there has been serious damage to the social life of areas and to the notion of community. This was well expressed by the government-appointed Urban Task Force, chaired by Richard Rogers, when it declared that there was a need to 'reclaim the potential of the "street" to meet many different community needs, as opposed simply to providing a conduit for motor vehicles' (Department of the Environment, Transport and the Regions 1999: 87). Money spent on serious traffic reduction measures in areas with high volumes of traffic would promote community life and increase social cohesion. It is telling that some of the most high-profile community action of the 1960s was against road building which it was felt would destroy city neighbourhoods. Even after the demolition the process of destruction of community has continued.

The production of cars was to prove one of the most influential forms of capitalist organization in the twentieth century. Henry Ford's ideas on boosting car production via the moving assembly line, whereby each worker could stay in the same place and perform the same task on each car, was a major advance on existing forms of production where cars were built one at a time from scratch. Later generations of sociologists were to christen this 'Fordism' in recognition of the fact that these techniques of mass production spread from the car industry to many sectors of manufacturing industry. As we have said, Ford saw the potential in the mass market for the car. This not only transformed the fortunes of his firm, making it the world's top car manufacturer, but also can be said to have transformed the nature of twentieth-century capitalism. Car industries around the world became important sources of employment, production and consumption especially after the 1950s.

The future: post car or new car?

Just as many millions more aspire to be motorists the grim impact of carbon emissions on global warming becomes more apparent.

A world which takes global warming seriously has to search for new ways of getting around which are not reliant on oil. Although in rich-world societies the car has supplanted other forms of mobility it can now be viewed as a dysfunctional technology and a post-petroleum-transport future is being discussed. The days of unlimited supplies of oil are coming to an end, which makes the future of the petrol-fuelled car problematic. Some commentators believe that the peak point for oil production has now been reached whereas others believe it is a few years away. Obviously, as oil is a finite resource then there must come a point at which production will peak. The high point for oil discoveries was in the 1960s. Whoever is right, the oil industry is now developing petroleum reserves which previously were regarded as too difficult to reach and too expensive (Roberts 2005). Oil production is linked to global politics, with two-thirds of the world supply currently coming from the Middle East (Gilbert and Perl 2008: 129). There are two main responses to the challenge of peak oil for personal transport: one is behavioural change and the other is a technological fix, meaning the substitution of alternative fuels for oil. Biofuels, hydrogen vehicles, electric battery vehicles are all being explored. Behavioural change, many more people moving to public transport and walking and cycling, is a more attainable goal in the short term. Governments can encourage mode switching by higher fuel taxes and using measures to encourage car sharing and less car use in general.

There can be little doubt that a personal form of transport is going to remain most people's choice but it seems inevitable that in the future it will not be powered by petrol. As this chapter should have demonstrated, there would be many advantages for communities and the environment if people were to travel less by car. A major benefit would be an improvement in personal and public health, and this is what the next chapter explores.

Further reading

Böhm, S., Jones, C., Land, C. and Paterson, M. (eds.) (2006). *Against Automobility*. Oxford: Blackwell. A stimulating collection of essays on aspects of car culture.

Dennis, K. and Urry, J. (2009). *After the Car*. Cambridge: Polity Press. An analysis of possible futures for personal transport.

Paterson, M. (2007). *Automobile Politics*. Cambridge: Cambridge University Press. An analysis of automobility from a political ecology perspective which seeks to understand how a post-car society can be constructed.

four

Life and death

How we travel has significant consequences for our bodies: car driving is sedentary travel which, in the context of a sedentary lifestyle, can be harmful, whereas walking and cycling are excellent forms of daily exercise which increases bodily fitness. Sadly there are more severe health consequences from the transport system, with just over 3,000 deaths and 26,000 serious injuries each year on UK roads (Milmo 2009). This level of death and injury constitutes a serious public health problem in the UK but one which for many years has not been given a high profile. The first part of this chapter examines the threats to health from the transport system – the decline of physical activity, the deaths and serious injuries from road traffic crashes and the pollutants which damage human health – and assesses how policy can respond. The second part explores the contribution that healthy transport – walking and cycling – can make to a healthy lifestyle and a healthier transport system. The chapter concludes with a discussion of the meaning of a healthy transport policy.

Obesity

Sedentary lifestyles pose a major challenge for health care today and obesity is a growing and serious health problem. The UK has the highest rate of obesity in the EU and is fast approaching the levels seen in the USA, the world leader in obesity rates. The changing nature of transport bears some of the responsibility as the physically active modes of cycling and walking have declined over the past half century and the sedentary mode of car driving has become the norm for adults. The associated decline in the use of public transport has contributed to a reduction in physical activity levels as most public transport journeys involve a walk to and from the bus stop or train station. The way we travel is just one of the reasons why obesity has increased so dramatically over the past thirty years: we can also cite poor diet, junk food advertising, cheap but unhealthy food, the decline of home cooking, the popularity of convenience foods and the introduction of the microwave together with the decline in shared meals and the rise of 'grazing'.

Obesity is defined as a body mass index of more than 30, which means that a person is more than 20 per cent overweight. Through the last quarter of the twentieth century UK obesity rates climbed. In 1980, 6 per cent of men and 8 per cent of women were obese. By 2004 the figure for both men and women was 24 per cent in England and Wales. The Scottish figures are higher but show a similar increase (*BBC News*, 6 June 2007; Davis et al. 2007). Alarmingly, the government-sponsored Foresight report on obesity trends predicts that by 2050 40 per cent of the UK population could be obese (Foresight 2007: 6). Obesity in adults makes them more vulnerable to a range of debilitating and chronic conditions. Childhood obesity is more serious as it can produce the early onset of coronary heart disease, diabetes and other serious health problems in adult life. Among boys aged 2 to 15 in England the obesity rate is 19 per cent while for girls in this age range the rate is 18 per cent (NHS Information Centre 2006).

Why there should have been a rise in obesity and an allied reduction in physical activity is not accounted for by one reason alone but results from a confluence of factors. Modern life has been designed to reduce physical exertion, and the extensive use of the car is part of this trend. Physical exertion has been reduced in the home: housework has been made easier with the use of the washing machine, the vacuum cleaner, the dishwasher and other appliances. When we note that the most popular leisure pursuit is television viewing, with the average person in the UK watching more than three hours of television a day, then it should not surprise us that obesity rates and levels of overweight have increased. We are as a nation taking in too many calories for a reduced level of physical activity. As Davis et al. (2007) point out, in pre-industrial times our ancestors would expend around 1,000 kilocalories (kcal) a day as physical activity and their intake of calories was typically 3,000 kcal a day. So the ratio of intake to expenditure as physical activity was 3:1. Nowadays we are on average consuming seven times as many kilocalories as we are expending in physical activity, that is to say, 2,100 kcal a day of food but only 300 kcal a day of physical expenditure. Davis et al. believe that the decline in physical activity rates among the UK population is mainly attributable to the fact that there is far less walking. Cycling has declined since the 1950s but as it now accounts for many fewer of the total journeys made it cannot be the main reason for this fall. The authors highlight the fact that:

- Main car drivers walk only half the distance and for half the time of adults in non-car owning households;

- This equates to a deficit of 56 minutes of walking every week for these drivers relative to adults in non-car households; and
- Over a decade we calculate that this could lead to a weight gain of more than 2 stones.

(Davis et al. 2007: 3)

There is some evidence that disadvantaged people are more likely to suffer obesity: 32 per cent of women in the poorest one-fifth of English households are obese compared with only 19 per cent of women in the richest one-fifth of households. Furthermore, children from the lowest-income households are almost twice as likely to be obese as children from the highest-income households (Sustrans 2008 citing NHS data).

Obesogenic environments

An obesogenic environment is one which encourages sedentary activities. It is 'the sum of influences that the surroundings, opportunities or conditions of life have on producing obesity in individuals or populations' (Swinburn and Figger in Jones et al. 2007: 9). These are environments where it is difficult to walk or cycle or too dangerous so to do, where facilities, work-places and homes have been organized to be as convenient as possible with the least expenditure of physical energy. Generally, housing and employ-ment will be built around access by car and, in some of the most obesogenic environments, the only access will be by car. The creation of out-of-town retail parks with free parking discourages physical activity, while new business parks, accessible only by car and with ample car parking, are another instance of the creation of an obesogenic environment. Further-more, the primary transport modes which expend physical energy – cycling and walking – are much more difficult and hazardous in a car-dominated environment. It is difficult to deny that the roads of Britain have become progressively more hostile to cyclists and pedestrians. The contribution that the organization of transport makes to the creation of obesogenic environ-ments is, in part, to do with the reduction of safe, public space in which to walk or cycle. Indeed, one of the main arguments used by parents to defend their decision to drive their children to school is that the roads and pave-ments are too dangerous for children to walk or cycle to school. It might be said that obesogenic environments follow naturally from a transport system which is built around the needs of the car and car drivers. In this car-dependent society that we have created, children naturally respond to the fears and anxieties of their parents so that many of them will not want to walk or cycle to school because they have been made only too well aware of the possible hazards. The growing fear in society over cycling had led to a generation of children not being allowed to use their bicycles as transport and consequently not burning off enough calories. Children's independent mobility has declined markedly while the 'school run' – what a misnomer this is – has become a routine part of many parents' lives, as has escorting children to many activities and places, often by car. (See Chapter 7.)

Overweight

Obesity is an all too visible sign of being overweight, but a focus on obesity should not mean that we forget the millions of people who are not obese but are overweight. One is overweight if one's body mass index is between 25 and 29. Being overweight puts one at greater risk of developing hypertension, coronary heart disease, type 2 diabetes and osteoarthritis (Cavill in Tolley 2003: 147–8).

Sedentary transport is part of a sedentary lifestyle in which sitting down to work has become much more prevalent. Certain sections of the population, mainly the better off, have responded by reinserting physical activity into their lives. Commonly this is done by joining a gym, leisure centre or health club. Nowadays there are thousands of people who drive to a health and fitness club to walk on a treadmill or cycle on an exercise bike and then drive home again.

Yet those on the lowest incomes are the most likely to be physically inactive: 44 per cent of women and 34 per cent of men in the poorest households in England are sedentary compared with only 33 per cent of women and 28 per cent of men in the wealthiest households (Craig and Mindell 2006).

Box 4.1 Health benefits of regular physical activity

Regular physical activity improves health in the following ways:

- Reduces the risk of dying prematurely
- Reduces the risk of dying prematurely from heart disease
- Reduces the risk of developing diabetes
- Reduces the risk of high blood pressure
- Reduces blood pressure in people who already have high blood pressure
- Reduces the risk of developing colon cancer
- Reduces feelings of depression and anxiety
- Helps control weight
- Helps build and maintain healthy bones, muscles and joints
- Helps older adults become stronger and better able to move about without falling
- Promotes psychological well-being

Source: Cavill in Tolley 2003, from US Department of Health and Human Services

Physical activity and government policy

The relationship between the physical environment and the range of economic and social forces which impinge on individual behaviour are complex.

Public health and transport policy

Before the 1990s the Ministry of Transport did not make connections between its work and health policy and the Department of Health did not address the transport implications of health policy. In the Conservative government's public health document *The Health of the Nation* published in 1993 the only mention of transport was in the document's focus on road traffic accidents and deaths, where a target was established for a reduction in both of these (Department of Health 1993). The break-through came the following year in 1994 when the Royal Commission on Environmental Pollution published a report on transport which detailed the injurious impact of the transport system on physical activity, air quality and other areas. Yet in 1995 the government's Physical Activity Task Force still ignored the role that car dependence played in the reduction of physical activity (Department of Health 1995). However, the new Labour government elected in 1997 made plain the connections between health and transport policy with the publication of its White Paper *A New Deal for Transport* in 1998, which declared: 'The way we travel is making us a less healthy nation' (Department of the Environment, Transport and the Regions 1998: 22). It listed the key negative health outcomes of transport as:

- Reduced levels of physical activity and association with coronary heart disease
- Premature deaths and hospital admissions associated with vehicle emissions
- Road traffic deaths and injuries
- Effect of traffic noise on sleep
- The increase in escorting children by car
- Inequalities caused by land-use planning

The Blair government's first public health White Paper *Our Healthier Nation*, published in 1998, was certain that

> An Integrated National Transport Policy ... will ensure a healthier environment for all, as part of our commitment to sustainable development. The strategy will tackle congestion and pollution and their damaging consequences, promote cleaner and safer vehicles, and greater use of public transport, cycling and walking. The health benefits will

include better air quality, improved levels of fitness, reduced levels of stress and fewer accidents.

(Department of Health 1998: 3.31)

These aspirations were encapsulated in public health policy and therefore issued as guidance to the local health services around the country. But these recommendations have to be set against what actually has happened over the past decade. Road traffic grew overall by 15 per cent, and by 27 per cent on motorways, in the decade to 2006 (Parkhurst and Dudley 2008: 57). The decline in overall levels of walking and cycling has continued. So despite government pressing the policy levers one could not conclude that we have a healthier transport system than when Labour came to power. Nonetheless there has been a great deal of activity at the local level. Some health authorities, for example, have given money to the transport department to support traffic calming, while others have provided money for the environmental transport organization Sustrans. These are both examples of cross-sector funding. Hospitals have tried to set a good example in many areas by charging for car parking and introducing schemes which will encourage their staff to use public transport or to walk or cycle to work. Transport and health professionals are working together on a number of schemes where public health and transport policy overlap.

The Wanless Report, commissioned in the wake of a substantial increase in health expenditure, analysed ways in which 'full engagement' by citizens in their own health would reduce the demand on health services in the future. The report, *Securing Good Health for the Whole Population*, published in 2004 highlighted the decrease in physical activity as one of the factors related to the onset of chronic diseases. Lack of physical activity is seen as an individual risk factor. The report called for more measures to encourage people to walk and cycle and to ensure that this happened in a safe environment with proper segregation between walkers/cyclists and the car. Wanless identified the greater use of cars for short journeys as one of the contributory factors to the reduced physical activity rate among the population (Wanless 2004).

It is understandable that government should be concerned about the decline in physical activity given the rapid increase in obesity levels, for not only is there a future cost to the NHS but it also represents a rising cost in the present. Although equal attention needs to be paid to energy intake, increased levels of physical activity would reduce the imbalance between calories consumed and energy expended. As a response to Wanless, the Department of Health produced *Choosing Health* in 2004, and this, together with the publication of *Choosing Activity* in 2005, aimed to increase the levels of physical activity in the population by making known the links between physical activity and improved health. *Choosing Activity* was a compendium of ideas on how local government, the NHS, voluntary

agencies and business could work together to promote increased physical activity. These Department of Health documents complemented the Department for Transport's *Walking and Cycling: An Action Plan* which set out a programme to increase walking and cycling by changes in land use, improving the local environment, tackling anti-social behaviour and upgrading the facilities for walking and cycling (Department for Transport 2004). Another clear connection between transport and health was seen in 2008 when the publication of the government's anti-obesity strategy, *Healthy Weight, Healthy Lives*, led to the announcement of a 'Walking into Health' campaign, aiming to get one-third of England walking at least 1,000 more steps daily by 2012 together with a 'Healthy Towns' programme in nine areas which aims to combat obesity with measures to increase physical activity and improve diets and nutrition (Department of Health 2008).

Air quality

Air pollution is a serious consequence of road traffic which has to be considered when one is examining the health consequences of our transport system. The quality of the air we breathe is important for human health: poor air quality can significantly reduce life expectancy, exacerbate respiratory conditions such as asthma and inhibit people from exercising in the open air (see Table 4.1). UK air is much cleaner than it was when coal was used for domestic heating, which resulted in photochemical smogs forming in some industrial cities that directly affected human life and sickness

Table 4.1 Health effects of air pollutants from vehicles

Pollutant	Effect
Nitrogen oxide	Irritation and inflammation of the lungs increasing susceptibility to viral infection, bronchitis and pneumonia.
PM10	Inflammation of lungs, worsening of symptoms in people with heart and lung conditions, linkage of long-term exposure to heart and lung conditions, linkage long-term exposure to coronary heart disease and lung cancer
Carbon monoxide	Prevention of normal transport of oxygen by blood, resulting in the reduction of oxygen supply to the heart
Ozone	Pain of deep breathing, coughing irritation and inflammation of lungs
Benzene	Associated with cancer, leukaemia and impotence
1,3 butadiene	Cause of cancer

Sources: Transport and Health Study Group 1991; Parliamentary Office of Science and Technology 2002 patterns. The London smog of 1952 is believed to have caused more than 4,000 deaths. Today, road traffic is a major cause of poor air quality, with excessive concentrations leading to extremely poor air quality in certain areas, particularly heavily trafficked inner-city districts. However, advances in technology have meant that each individual new car produces less pollution than was the case ten years ago. The Air Quality Expert Group estimates that poor air quality reduces life expectancy in the UK by an average of seven to eight months (Air Quality Expert Group 2007a: 7).

The government's Air Quality Strategy is implemented via local authorities and informed by regulations from the EU. If air pollution in an area administered by a local authority reaches a certain level then the local authority has to designate this an air quality management area.

Given the expected increases in traffic levels the Royal Commission on Environmental Pollution concludes that air pollution from road transport will continue to be a problem especially in urban areas. The costs are substantial. The last estimate made of the impact of air pollution on life expectancy was that in the year 1995/96 it was responsible for around 24,000 premature deaths (Parliamentary Office of Science and Technology 2002: 1). Air quality improvement is a partial success story. In the ten years up to 2007 pollutants from road transport reduced by around 50 per cent and the expectation is that they will continue to fall by 25 per cent over the next decade (Air Quality Expert Group 2007a: 28). This is encouraging yet the dilemma is that even though this progress has been made these gains are outweighed by the continuing rise in vehicle numbers.

Table 4.2 Transport measures to reduce air pollutants from vehicles

Measure	*Effect*
Use of new technologies, hybrid vehicles, hydrogen from natural gas or renewables from burnt petrol vehicles fitted with nitrogen oxide traps	Reduces carbon dioxide emissions for each kilometre travelled and also emissions of nitrogen oxide and particulate matter
Increased use of diesel instead of petrol in engines	Reduces carbon dioxide but increases particulate matter and nitrogen oxide
Use of biofuel for transport	Reduces carbon dioxide but may lead to increased emissions of ammonia, nitrous oxide and volatile organic compounds
Demand management/behavioural change Improved public transport coupled with disincentives for private car usage	Reduces emissions of both types of pollutant

Source: Derived from Air Quality Expert Group 2007b: table 2

The reduction of carbon dioxide emissions will contribute not only to climate change targets but also improve air quality. In 2004, road traffic was responsible for around 28 per cent of the UK's total carbon dioxide emissions (Steer Davies Gleave 2006: 1.9). In transport the key ways in which pollution can be reduced are fuel switching, using a less polluting fuel, managing demand, as for example with a congestion charge, or getting people to change their travel behaviour, for example cycling to work rather than using the car (Table 4.2). It is not always possible to hit both the targets of carbon dioxide reduction and improving air quality. The use of diesel makes this clear: the switch to diesel means there are lower carbon dioxide emissions yet diesel produces more particulate matter and nitrogen oxide so the amount of air pollutants increases (Air Quality Expert Group 2007b).

Road deaths and serious injuries

Road casualties – deaths or serious injuries – constitute a major global health problem. Indeed, the World Health Organization (2004b) estimates that by 2020 road deaths could be the world's third major killer.

Box 4.2 Road crashes

- Every three minutes a child is killed on the world's roads.
- Road deaths in poorer countries are set to rise by 80 per cent by 2020.
- More than 80 per cent of all deaths and 90 per cent of disability adjusted life years lost from road traffic injuries occur in developing countries.
- Road crashes are the biggest killer of young people in the EU and USA. Only HIV/AIDS kills more young men worldwide.
- Road crashes kill on the scale of malaria and tuberculosis.
- Road crashes kill 3,000 people worldwide every day.

Sources: Nantulya and Reich 2002; World Health Organization 2004b

---

Road crashes are the leading cause of death and admission to hospital for those under the age of 45 in EU countries (Breen 2002: 1109). In the UK there has been some real progress on reducing the death toll. As can be seen from Figure 4.1 the annual death toll has reduced despite the increase in the number of motor vehicles on the nation's roads. In 2007 just under 3,000 people were killed on Britain's road which was an achievement considering the year on year increase in traffic. Between 1980 and 2007 road traffic increased by 87 per cent yet the number of fatal and serious road crash casualties declined by 64 per cent (Department for Transport 2009c: 91). Yet it still remained the case in 2006/07 that more than three times as many

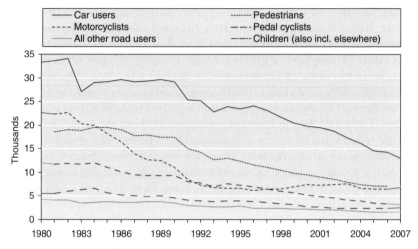

Figure 4.1 People killed or seriously injured in road accidents, Great Britain, 1980–2007

Source: Department for Transport 2009c: 91

people are killed on the roads as are murdered (figures on homicides from Office for National Statistics 2007; Travis 2008).

But this reduction in road deaths comes, it is argued, at the cost of a greatly increased level of fear regarding use of the roads by non-motorists which, in part, accounts for the decline in walking and cycling. This fear would appear to lie behind the reluctance of many parents to let their children walk or cycle to school or to see their friends or use local facilities on their own.

The advances in medical techniques for dealing with road injuries now mean that lives are saved where death would have resulted in the past, but this can mean that some victims survive with serous disabilities which they and their families have to cope with for the rest of their lives. Among these are those who suffer brain injuries which can mean that the personality of the victim changes or that they lose certain key aspects of cognitive functioning such as memory. Understandably this is distressing for families and friends who may find themselves living with a different person from the one they knew before the accident.

Road safety or road danger?

Death and serious injuries on the roads have reduced since the extremely high figures reached in the 1930s. In 1934, 7,343 people were killed, the highest number of road deaths in Britain in the twentieth century relative to population size and the number of vehicles on the road. Around 50 per cent of these were pedestrians (Dean 1947). In large part, the subsequent reduction has occurred because of the introduction of a series of measures which are now commonplace but at the time incurred the opposition and displeasure of motoring organizations: the driving test, speed limits and the pedestrian crossing. To keep this in perspective one must remember that in 1934 there were only a quarter of a million cars on the roads (Davis 1992). Today, with around 28 million cars on the road, there are on average about half the deaths of 1934, i.e. around 3,000. (If the 1934 death rate had continued then, with 28 million cars, we could expect an annual death toll of 822,416.) In recent decades there have been marked improvements in reducing the death toll. In the mid-1960s there were 8,000 deaths a year on the roads – and the fall in deaths since then is mainly attributable to drink drive legislation and compulsory seat belt wearing.

In 2006 there were just over 3,000 deaths and 237,000 injuries and the annual cost was estimated to be £470 million for the NHS and £7.2 billion for the economy (Audit Commission 2007: 8). However, the UK has a lower rate of death and serious injury than many other European countries.

Road deaths affect almost all of us in some way (see Figure 4.2). 'One in every 200 deaths is on the roads, including a quarter of the deaths of men aged 15–24. During a lifetime, people have a one in 20 chance of serious injury; most know someone who has died on our roads' (Audit Commission 2007: 8). There is a tendency to hide this form of death. It can be argued that local authorities who insist on removing roadside memorials set up by grieving family when their loved one has been killed are doing just that. The local

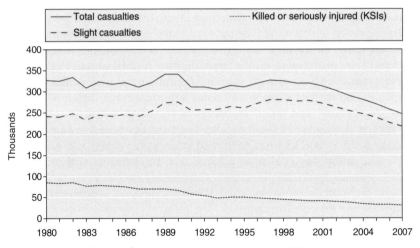

Figure 4.2 Road casualties, Great Britain, 1980–2007

Source: Department for Transport 2009c: 90

authorities believe that drivers will be distracted by these memorials and hence when they remove them are acting to prevent further accidents. The legal system too is felt to be at fault. There are numerous testimonies from the bereaved stating that they believe the sentencing process does not sufficiently recognize the seriousness of road traffic offences which result in death and serious injury.

Traditional road safety education was aimed at pedestrians, cyclists and the more vulnerable road users, particularly children. This has undoubtedly made non-motorists much more careful around cars because of the dangers they pose. Clearly, training for small children on how to cross the road and for older children on how to cycle safely is essential. Yet the ideology of road safety has been criticized because it inculcates undue deference to cars and the belief that roads belong to them allied with a tendency to 'blame the victim' (Davis 1992). Above all, traditional road safety education accepts that the hegemony of the car is here to stay so that people must adapt to it. An example of this is the driver awareness classes which some local authorities promote in schools for 16- and 17-year-olds. The evidence, however, reveals that the classes encourage children to start driving earlier than they would have done, which puts them at greater risk because of the high casualty rate among teenage drivers (Roberts 2001; World Health Organization 2008).

The Road Danger Reduction Forum provides a different perspective on road safety, arguing that the real danger on the roads comes from motor vehicles and their drivers so that these need to be the focus of educational and safety campaigns. Measures advocated to reduce 'road danger' include traffic engineering which would make it more difficult to speed in residential areas, stricter enforcement of existing speed limits and the introduction of 20 miles per hour zones in all residential areas (Davis 1992). This is similar to the approach which would see the road crash in the context of the overall decisions made concerning the speed limit on the road, the design of the road and law enforcement on the road. In other words, to focus exclusively on the crash itself provides an incomplete and partial understanding. This perspective holds that most road deaths are preventable using a series of traffic engineering and speed enforcement measures which would ensure safe speeds alongside safety education. The most developed example of this thinking is the Swedish Vision Zero road safety policy which was adopted in 1997. The ambitious goal is to achieve zero road deaths and injuries on Sweden's roads by 2020. This aims consciously to move away from the focus on the road user to seeing road deaths and injuries as preventable if the entirety of the process is examined. The clear assumption is that the road builders, the traffic engineers, the automobile industry all have a responsibility in relation to the road death and injury toll. 'Rather than emphasising the responsibility of the road user alone, Vision Zero explicitly states that responsibility is shared both by the system designers and the road user'

(Whitelegg and Haq 2006: 8). The intention is to achieve a cultural shift in relation to road deaths whereby road deaths are as unacceptable as deaths from air or train crashes.

Who dies?

There is a clear social class gradient in road deaths, with those in social class 5 more likely to die than those in social class 1. The injury mortality rate among children of unemployed parents is thirteen times that for the most affluent group, while deaths for pedestrian injuries were twenty times higher (Edwards et al. 2006). As Green and Edwards (2008) point out, this higher rate of death is because many of these children are walking and cycling, rather than travelling as car passengers, and so are exposed to greater danger. An important move would be to reduce the speed and volume of traffic (ibid.: 184). Indeed, the observation in the World Health Organization/ World Bank report on road deaths in developing countries also applies to those on the lowest incomes in this country: 'They benefit the least from policies designed for motorized travel, but bear a disproportionate share of the disadvantages of motorization and in terms of injury, pollution and the separation of communities' (World Health Organization 2004b: 10).

The issue of speed and its control has become a controversial topic in recent years with the introduction of safety (speed) cameras. Speeding has been a tolerated offence for some time: the police do not take action against motorists who exceed the speed limit by only a couple of miles an hour. Too often this means that drivers are routinely travelling through built-up urban areas at 35 mph which is not a safe speed from the viewpoint of pedestrians using the road – see Table 4.3. (Ninety-five per cent of pedestrian road deaths are in urban areas.) Department for Transport figures show that 50 per cent of cars exceeded the 30 mph speed limit and 27 per cent exceeded the 40 mph limit in 2006 (Department for Transport 2007d). The flouting of speed limits extends to buses and lorries as well. Speeding – defined as exceeding the speed limit whether it is by one mile or by ten or

Table 4.3 Average chance of surviving a collision if you are struck by a car while walking or cycling

Vehicle speed mph	Chance of survival %	Cars exceeding that speed in built-up areas %
20	95	95
30	45	72
40	5	12

Source: Adapted from Slower Speeds Initiative 2000

more – is an offence where detection is low. Speeding is a major contributory factor in around one-third of fatal road crashes, which amounts to around 1,000 deaths in a year. Reducing average speeds by 1 mph cuts the average crash frequency by around 5 per cent (Corbett 2003: 104, 105).

Speed cameras have become a controversial issue in the past few years, with a determined campaign against their use by the Association of British Drivers. Yet studies have shown that at camera sites casualties have fallen by 22 per cent and 42 per cent fewer people have been killed or seriously injured (Clement 2006).

The control of speed in urban areas is particularly important if there is to be a growth in cycling and walking, as many people are reluctant to walk or cycle in areas where traffic speeds are high. This has led to a number of local authorities introducing 20 mph speed limits in urban areas. In the light of the evidence on how many drivers ignore speed limits, if speeds are to be kept below 20 mph in these areas there are two options. One is for enforcement by the police, which is not a feasible option in most parts of the country where the police do not regard traffic law enforcement as a priority. The other is to redesign the area so that exceeding the speed limit becomes much more difficult for drivers. Home Zones illustrate how this can be done: they are small areas in towns and cities where pavements have been built out to allow more safe space for pedestrians, where cars are restricted by narrowing the roads and where environmental improvements such as tree planting encourage people to walk, to sit and to meet one another. There are also clear environmental benefits from speed enforcement and reduction. A properly enforced 70 mph limit would cut carbon emissions from road transport by nearly 1 million tonnes of carbon per annum, while a 60 mph limit would almost double this reduction (Anable et al. 2006b).

Walking

The health benefits of walking are many and various. Walking is something that most people, with the exception of those in wheelchairs and frail elderly people, are able to do. It does not require special equipment and there is no joining fee to start walking. Walking is a good aerobic exercise and has proven benefits for most people. It uses the major muscle groups of the legs, is regular and rhythmic, one can make it load bearing, vary the intensity and it burns off calories.

The government's advice to the adult population to engage in half an hour a day of physical exercise is most easily met by walking. The National Heart Forum estimates that if walking for this length of time each day was widely adopted by those who take no exercise at present then there would be a significant reduction in coronary heart disease, a major killer in the UK (Cavill in Tolley 2003: 146).

For more than a decade government and local authorities have declared that cycling and walking should be encouraged and promoted. As we have seen, this was a belated conversion as for much of the post-war period transport policy has been organized to accommodate the car. Many critics of the dominant transport orthodoxy believed that cities and urban areas were being reorganized in order to prioritize the needs of the car. Walking was only recognized as a transport mode in the 1990s when the Conservative government belatedly, in the wake of creating a cycling strategy, decided that it should do the same for walking. The Conservatives bequeathed this 'walking strategy' to the Labour government in 1997 and it was announced that it was to be a 'daughter document' of the Integrated Transport White Paper. But it never appeared and it would seem that this was because the Labour government just could not see how it would be able to 'spin' the document without the press producing pictures of John Cleese and the Ministry of Silly Walks from Monty Python! The government downgraded its walking strategy to merely advice to local authorities on walking. This was followed up by *On the Move by Foot* (Department for Transport 2003b), a discussion document aimed at local authority and health staff to promote thinking as to how walking could be promoted.

Yet what has happened to walking? Sadly the answer is that it has continued to decline as a transport mode. The *Health Survey for England 2004* shows that only 35 per cent of men and 24 per cent of women take sufficient physical activity to attain health benefits. There has been an 18 per cent decline in levels of walking between 1989/91 and 2004 as measured by annual distance travelled on foot – from 237 to 196 miles per year. In the same period the number of trips made on foot per year declined by 25 per cent – from 328 to 246. Women walk slightly more frequently than men, making 27 per cent of trips on foot compared with 23 per cent for men (Department for Transport 2005b: 18).

The reasons for this decline in walking are not difficult to find. Walking has been designed out of many people's lives and the areas where they live. In large part, people walked more in the past because they needed to reach certain destinations or, as users of public transport, to walk at least part of the way.

In a car-dependent society this is no longer true as the walking has been taken out of the journey. It is much more attractive to walk with a purpose, for walking to be part of the business of conducting one's life. But if the local shops have closed down, the post office has shut, the bank moved elsewhere or online then many people cannot reach facilities on foot even if they wanted to. In suburban areas numerous roads have not been designed with walking to a destination in mind. For many people their only use of the pavement is to cross it on their way to the car. Given these restrictions it makes it difficult for some people to walk more without making a conscious effort.

Other factors are relevant in looking at the reasons why there is less walking. We can include fear, fear of traffic or just fear of certain streets and locations which are not safe for people to walk because of crime, or at least that is their perception.

Despite all these reservations, given the high number of journeys made which are less than one mile there remains a substantial number of journeys which could be undertaken on foot.

Box 4.3 Walkability

The degree to which a single route, or a system of routes, between points is relatively short, barrier free, interesting, safe, well-lighted, comfortable and inviting to pedestrians.

(Schöppe and Braubach 2007)

The decline of walking is a product of the degree of car dependence that has been created in our society. As Freund and Martin (2004: 274) point out, walking contests the dominant notions of time and space which have been structured around speed and convenience which can only be provided by the car. Housing developments are usually designed on the understanding that all households will have the use of a car so that facilities are often just not within walking reach. In these areas it becomes much more difficult to insert a walking journey into one's daily routine as a car is needed just to pick up a carton of milk or a newspaper. Certain street layouts and neighbourhood designs are much more conducive to walking journeys than others. Unfortunately a great deal of post-war suburban building has been on the assumption that most people living on estates will have access to a car: it is low-density and spread out. Barton believes that the reason why so much post-war housing has taken the form of the suburban semi has been the conservatism of house builders and property developers (Barton in Cavill 2007: 13). Another factor has been the planners' preference for single-use development, with cities zoned for residential or commercial or industrial development so that the areas where employment is located are separate from where people live. This has the disadvantage of creating suburbs which are at some distance from jobs. In contrast, the following factors have been found to increase the level of cycling and walking:

- High densities
- A greater mixture of land uses
- A balance between housing and jobs
- Pedestrian and cycle friendly site and street design
- Grid street networks.

(Sustrans 2007a)

These findings demonstrate the close relationship that has to exist between transport, environment and society if healthier outcomes are to be produced.

Cycling

Given the knowledge that we now have about the impact of carbon emissions on the environment and the impact of sedentary transport on our bodies it is unfortunate that the bicycle was invented before the car and is being supplanted by the car around the world. The move from independent mobility by bicycle to car which took place in the UK in the 1950s is now transforming the transport systems of China and India and other developing countries.

As a transport machine the bicycle has many advantages. It is environmentally friendly – it produces no noise or fumes. It provides door-to-door transport. It is cheap and can be used to access public transport. The bicycle provides excellent exercise and has a positive impact on health.

The British Medical Association report on cycling spells this out:

> It is potentially one of the most appropriate ways for individuals to maintain their fitness through the rhythmic contraction and relaxation of the large limb muscles. In contrast to running and jogging, which can place high stress on hips, knees, ankles and the Achilles tendons, there is very little risk of cycling leading to overstrain of muscles, ligaments or other injuries from 'overuse', particularly as the body is supported on a saddle, with pressure and effort distributed between two hands, two feet and one backside.
>
> (British Medical Association 1992: 16)

Regular cycling can help protect against the risk of coronary heart disease, strokes and late onset diabetes in adults. It also has a role to play in building and maintaining healthy bones, muscles and joints (Cavill and Davis 2007).

Yet cycling accounts for only 1 per cent of all personal journeys and 2 per cent of all personal mileage (Department for Transport 2007d) so there is a great deal of potential to increase cycling journeys among the population.

The National Cycling Strategy published in 1996 set out a target of quadrupling cycling – on 1996 figures – by 2012 with recommendation to local authorities that they too publish cycling strategies which would enable them to increase the amount of cycling in their areas. The quadrupling of cycle journeys by the 2012 target has since been dropped as too ambitious. It is important to consider why this should have occurred. Cycling is but one part of the transport picture, and many people see the ever-increasing number of cars on the roads as a disincentive to use their bicycle. It is instructive to compare the national picture with London where cycling has increased by around 50 per cent since 2000. The congestion charge and better provision for cyclists have been important in achieving this.

In considering the health impact of cycling, safety is a major problem. A judgement has to be made between the undoubted health benefits of cycling and the risks involved in cycling on busy roads. Before cars reached a certain density on the roads it was possible for cars and bicycles to share the highway. Increased speed of cars means that some motorists become impatient when they are required to slow down because of a bicycle. Examining the reasons why people do not cycle or do not cycle more, one quickly comes across safety as a major reason. Almost half of respondents – 47 per cent – to a national survey agreed with the statement that 'the idea of cycling on busy roads frightens me' (Department for Transport 2007d). With the roads becoming more hostile for bicycles the unfortunate, but understandable, result is that numbers of cyclists now cycle on the pavements. This is hazardous for pedestrians, particularly frail, elderly people, and each year there are serious injuries and in some years even a small number of deaths as a result. For instance, three pedestrians were killed by cyclists in 2005 and there were 61 serious injuries (Department for Transport 2006a: 84).

Countries which have increased the number of cycle journeys, such as the Netherlands and Sweden, have produced a network of cycle routes which are segregated from traffic and the road ensuring that cyclists do not have to negotiate with cars for road space. All too often in the UK cycle lanes are no more than a continuous white line on the side of the road which clearly does not afford protection against the traffic.

As around 40 per cent of cycling trips are to and from work, employers have a part to play in encouraging cycle use by providing facilities such as showers and proper bicycle storage facilities. However, overall only 3 per cent of commuting trips are made by bicycle (Department for Transport 2007d). Looking at trips on the National Cycle Network, 12 per cent were commuting journeys in 2007 with the average commuting distance being just under five miles, the same as two-thirds of car journeys to work (Sustrans 2007b: 7).

Transport and health

Transport has a key role to play in improving the health of the population.

Lack of physical activity is one of the reasons for the increase in obesity and this is a major challenge for government which will take a number of decades to overcome. The NHS obviously has a key role to play in this. Many believe that its staff should set an example to the rest of us by using healthy modes of transport wherever possible and cutting back on car use. This is not obvious to all those working in the NHS, however. Some years ago the NHS decided to introduce parking charges in hospital car parks, designed in part to encourage a shift from car use to public transport by visitors to hospitals and the staff who work there. In 2008 it was decided by the Scottish government, swiftly followed by Wales, that these charges would be abolished, leaving them in place only in England. Those patients who have to visit hospital on a frequent basis are obviously penalized by this policy. On the other hand, abolition of the charges means that money for the upkeep of car parks has to come from other NHS budgets. There is also the issue of the contribution of hospital-related traffic to global warming. The NHS as a whole – buildings, staff and patient travel, procurement – generates 30 per cent of total public sector carbon emissions and 2.7 per cent of total carbon dioxide emissions for the UK.

Walking and cycling are inexpensive ways to improve general health and fitness and increase life expectancy. But as we have seen, they need to be promoted and supported through policy initiatives where local authorities, the NHS and voluntary organizations have to work together to effect a shift in the transport culture which would prioritize these two modes. Alongside this, there is surely a strong case for speed reduction measures to accompany promotion of walking and cycling. As Corbett (2003) argues, a cultural shift is required which will recognize that speeding is a criminal offence which endangers lives and needs to be treated much more seriously.

Drivers: men, women and transport

When Barbara Castle became the first female transport minister in 1965 there was an outcry from some sections of the press when it was discovered that she was not a driver. In the 1960s this was something Barbara Castle had in common with most women in the UK. In comparison, forty years later when Ruth Kelly – who is a driver – was appointed to head the Department for Transport, 63 per cent of women were drivers (Department for Transport 2008b). Four decades ago it was still the case in most households that men were the drivers and women the passengers. In those days car manufacturers would drape female models over the bonnets of new cars at the Motor Show each year. Feminism has had its impact on the motor industry as it has on the workforce; however, public transport and public spaces have not changed sufficiently to meet the needs of men and women who are not using cars.

This chapter outlines the differences between men and women in their use of transport. The major change in the area of gender and transport has been the increasing access to cars by women, and one aim of this chapter is to show the resulting benefits but also the inequalities that have resulted. For all those who cannot drive, public transport is a residual form of transport, but here too there are important gender differences. Both men and women experience fear in certain parts of the public transport system and at particular times of the day, so we can ask how important is fear as a deterrent to moving to a more sustainable transport system? As well as considering this question the chapter examines the ways in which public spaces would need to change to make them safer for both men and women. The chapter ends with a discussion of the ways in which driving relates to caring and social justice.

Men and cars

There has been an association between masculinity and motor cars since the invention of the internal combustion engine. Numerous motor and car magazines have a mainly male readership and the overwhelming majority of motorsport enthusiasts are men. To make the connection quite clear, there is even a Men and Motors television channel. *Top Gear* is one of the most popular television programmes, in which Jeremy Clarkson and his fellow male presenters road test various cars, putting them through their paces (Grahame 1908). One could reasonably assume that the majority of viewers are men although the BBC disputes this, citing audience research that half its viewers are women (Plunkett 2005). It is still the case that men are more likely to travel as a driver than as a passenger.

The car originated as a vehicle for the rich who did not have to get their hands dirty by tinkering with the engine or even driving it, as they employed a (male) chauffeur. In Edwardian England and before the First World War, motorists were regarded as something of a public nuisance as they were often guilty of driving at speeds which endangered the lives of pedestrians. Toad of Toad Hall in Kenneth Grahame's *The Wind in the Willows* (1908) is a satire which reflected this attitude. The inter-war period saw the car lose its status as rich man's transport, the prerogative of the upper class, when men from the middle class became motorists. O'Connell (1998: 64) comments: 'For the middle class male engaged in professional or commercial activity, the model of car he drove made a statement about his success in the masculine world of work'. Interestingly, the 1920s and 1930s was also the era which was the high point of working-class male cycling, and male independent mobility of this kind can be seen to have been a precursor to the working-class man's car ownership which began in the 1950s.

Male teenage drivers are those most at risk of having a crash and this would appear to be bound up with their greater propensity to take risks when behind the wheel of a car. Redshaw (2008) has deemed this young male style of driving as one where the demonstration of driving skill is given precedence over caution. Although she is describing Australian young men, what she says rings true when she comments that the types of masculinity that get the most emphasis among young men are those that 'place a high value on risk taking, bravado, skilled performance with machines, rule-breaking and other forms of challenging authority and convention' (Redshaw 2008: 81 quoting Vick 2003). Redshaw uses the term 'combustion masculinity' to describe this explosive desire, which some young men have, to express themselves through cars. Among the young men that Redshaw studied she found that many thought that they had a 'natural' connection with cars. There was also a difference in how young men and women talked about cars and driving. The young men would talk about driving 'as you feel like' or 'doing whatever you want' with a car while the young women valued the independence and the time to themselves which the vehicle gave them (Redshaw 2008: 86). Significantly, some of these male attitudes did not seem to persist with men aged 23 or so, contrasting their more careful attitudes with those that they had five years earlier.

Joyriding is the most overt, aggressive and criminal of male connections with the car and has been predominantly associated with youths in deprived areas. Joyriding had become a popular activity with some young males as far back as the 1920s as under the Road Traffic Act 1930 taking and driving away other people's cars became an offence.

However, in a study of joyriding in Belfast since the 1930s O'Connell has shown that 37 per cent of Belfast offenders were from middle-class backgrounds in the inter-war period (O'Connell 2006: 458). That was an era when motor cars were a scarce commodity for the middle class, unlike today when in many families there is an expectation of owning a car at age 17. Corbett summarizes the social profile of contemporary joyriders: 'The backdrop to car theft for most known offenders seems to be a socially deprived home life, poverty, unemployment, underachievement and low aspirations located within a lower socioeconomic environment' (Corbett 2003: 53).

Joyriding and racing cars at high speeds along public roads are exhibitionistic displays of young males' fascination with cars and speed. More affluent males can display this via the purchase of high status cars. This too can have serious implications because of the high speeds which these vehicles can reach. Vanderbilt (2008) notes that men in the USA and many other countries have a higher propensity to die in road crashes, even taking into account the fact that they drive more than women. The problem seems to lie in the fact that men drive more aggressively which means they are more likely to crash (ibid.: 255). The World Health Organization report on road deaths and injuries shows that, country by country, between 66 per cent and 90 per cent of road deaths are male (World Health Organization 2004b: table A4; Redshaw 2008: 271). Men are also the prime perpetrators of 'road rage', when motorists exhibit extremely aggressive behaviour towards others, usually other motorists; often it seems born out of a frustration with the stresses and strains of driving in a congested urban environment. In an RAC report on the topic, 'anti-social, ill-tempered, foolish or violent behaviours' include 'headlight-flashing, tailgating, cutting in, obscene gestures, obstruction, verbal abuse, running over offending drivers or pedestrians, using various objects to smash windscreens, stabbing with screwdrivers and knives, spraying with ammonia, threatening with guns, poking, punching, throttling, beating' (Michael 2001: 59). Michael notes that the RAC argues that people who indulge in road rage have been 'dehumanized' by their experience of the frustrations of the contemporary motoring environment: congestion, delays, roadworks. The RAC claims that as the car is an extension of the home, it is personal territory, thus some motorists become violent when they believe that it has been invaded (Michael 2001: 62).

Michael points out that what has been ignored in these analyses is the car itself. For him the driver and the car fuse to become a hybrid so that the sentiment 'When I get into a car my character changes' has the obverse 'When I get into a car the car changes'.

There are many kinds of masculinity, with 'combustion masculinity' being only one of them, and it would seem sensible that aggressive images of driving and car use are not popularized. One of the reasons why *Top Gear* comes under criticism is that some feel that it glamourizes speed and risk taking which has led to calls for the BBC to take it off the air (Plunkett 2005). But how far does one go with this criticism? Computer games such as 'Grand Theft Auto', where players gain points by causing death and destruction amid the traffic in the city, would also be likely candidates for censorship if this logic was to apply. Yet there are other forms of masculinity and it may well be that the association between men and motors is declining for it was reported in 2008 that 'British blokes are losing their masculinity with many of them more comfortable ironing than they are under a car bonnet, according to a new survey' (*Metro*, 29 May 2008).

Whether men are 'losing their masculinity' because they prefer to spend less time tinkering with car engines is a moot point – and not many details were given of the survey. Certainly the computerized circuits of the modern car make it less possible for amateurs to fix and repair them.

Women and cars

The distribution of driving licences in the first half of the twentieth century reflected the gender inequalities of society. This is not to deny that after the First World War, aristocratic, eccentric and generally well heeled women took up driving. For them, as for subsequent generations of women, the car represented freedom, the freedom to go wherever they wanted (Pugh 2008: 253). In the Second World War, women became drivers both in the armed forces and also on the home front where women bus drivers were a common sight. But this employment did not survive the war; when mass motoring made its appearance in this country in the 1950s the family car was usually the preserve of the man. In the 1950s, with a majority of women at home, their principal role was to care for the children and to look after their household and their husband. The most important social change of the past fifty years is arguably the large-scale entry of women into the labour force. Women, as they entered the labour market, needed to access jobs in the same way as men, so car ownership became desirable.

Overall in the UK women still lag behind men in their possession of a driving licence: 63 per cent of women hold one while among men the figure is 80 per cent. This figure for men has remained stable since the mid-1990s, but for women possession of a licence has increased from 57 per cent in

1995/97 to 63 per cent in 2007. Within this figure the National Travel Survey shows that there has been a big increase in the number of older women holding a driving licence. From the mid-1990s to 2007 the percentage of women in the 60–69 age group with a licence increased from 45 per cent to 63 per cent, while in the over 70 age group the proportion of women with licences increased from 21 per cent to 36 per cent. As the survey points out, these percentages can be expected to carry on rising as younger women, with their higher rates of licence holding, reach retirement age (Department for Transport 2008b).

There is a difference between the purpose of trips before age 60 and after age 60. After 60, shopping, personal business and visiting friends become the main purpose of trips. This highlights the nature of gender inequality, with women still taking the major responsibility for children and shopping. As might be expected, women make a greater proportion of shopping trips whereas men make more commuting journeys. Escort education – taking children to school – is mainly undertaken by women in their 30s, and note that they make five times as many of these journeys as men do. Women in the age range 30–39 also make almost twice as many other escort trips.

The percentage of households with two or more cars has increased from 25 per cent in the mid-1990s to 32 per cent in 2007 (Department for Transport 2008b). This has increased the availability of cars for women in these households as they now have their own car rather than being secondary drivers in single-car households.

Consumption and the car

The car is the consumer object *par excellence*. It denotes social status, freedom, the individual lifestyle. It is also a gendered object: cars have looks which appeal to males and those which appeal to women. Edwards (2000) argues that there are three aspects to the gendering of consumption. First there is the gendering of objects designed solely for one sex, and here he gives the example of fast, exclusive cars to which we can now add cars styled with women in mind (although manufacturers have been a long time catching up with women's motoring and it was not until the late twentieth century that the first car designed by and specifically for women appeared). Second, gendering of consumer products, as with pink labels or the shape of an object. Third, the gendering of production (Edwards 2000: 132). The classic studies of car workers, for example, are studies of men in Dagenham or Halewood: Goldthorpe et al.'s study *The Affluent Worker* (1968) and Huw Beynon's *Working for Ford* (1973). This gendering is not immutable. An increasing number of women like to drive fast and choose cars that enable them to do so. Redshaw (2008) reports from Australia that the kind of driving associated with 'combustion masculinity' is now increasingly seen among young women.

With the onset of ethical consumption it might soon be the case that what is in your garage might be said to be as important as what is in your wardrobe, with electric cars or hybrids becoming the ethical choice. The car is the embodiment of the consumer society in the sense that not only do the more than 30 million vehicles on the roads transport their occupants they also, like the clothes we wear, say something about their drivers. The backlash against 4 × 4s is perhaps an early illustration of a more ethical attitude. Advertisers would want to persuade us that their car is a statement about social status or expression of individuality but we can also view the way in which we use cars in a more critical manner. The queue of vehicles at the traffic lights belching out fumes but with only one person in them might be said to be a statement about how much we all care about carbon emissions. The traffic jams around school gates in the morning and the afternoon tell us something about the extent to which walking and cycling have become an unusual event in many children's lives. Many people must have these thoughts as they wait in their cars to pick up their children from school or join a queue of cars waiting to get into a car park, but the contemporary organization of time and space, built around the flexibility and convenience of the car, often rules out other options.

Although some research suggests that many women regard cars in a different way from the way that many men do, women tending to see them primarily as a vehicle to get from A to B and less as a symbol of one's sexuality or importance, there is accumulating evidence that the onset of consumerism has changed this, with more women being interested in the look, the colour, the specifications and the speed of the vehicle. As women become more materially independent with a greater status in the labour market they are becoming more like men in their driving behaviour (Redshaw 2008). Many women, perhaps more than men, have feelings towards their cars. Although not making a point about gender, Sheller (2003: 2) argues that the era of automobility in which we live means that there are 'feelings, passions and embodied experiences' associated with being a driver. Women's role in car purchase is an important one, with one estimate being that they purchase 65 per cent of all new cars and influence about 60 per cent of all car sales (Sutton 2008). While not quite a fashion item, the look, the feel, the sound system are all important considerations when purchasing a vehicle.

For many women, given the fear that they experience in public spaces, especially after dark, their car not only gives them the ability to travel independently but also offers them a private space which makes them feel secure. This is an important consideration for it enables many women to have a social life and travel independently and for that reason it is understandable that they place a high value on their car. As we have seen, the car is viewed as a necessity for independent living in most parts of the country by the majority of people in this society, therefore to be carless is a handicap. This can start at an early age. Certainly both young men and women drivers in Carrabine and Longhurst's study in Manchester all saw the car as very important for their social networks (Carrabine and Longhurst 2002).

Women with cars and women without cars

The car is now a key technology for many women who have the primary care giver role in the family, whether that be for children or for elderly relations. Men are more likely to use their car for work whereas women are more likely to use it for a range of functions such as escorting children, doing the shopping, visiting relations.

Many households now require two incomes and two cars. If both partners are working, two cars may be essential when workplaces are at a distance. The spread of out-of-town office parks has made travel to work by public transport very difficult, sometimes impossible, for many people. Two jobs and two cars enable some families with children to drive their children not to the nearest school but another one they have chosen for its superior reputation or academic success. The car is the technology which enables many women to keep their life together, enabling them to drop children off at school, to visit the supermarket, to escort children, to keep in touch with a relative. After-school activities – ballet, football, learning a musical instrument – become much more feasible with the aid of a car but they add to the time poverty of many mothers' lives, as escorting is largely a female task. The car is a very useful addition to the tools that women can utilize in their daily lives because it enables time to be saved. Time poverty – a shortage of time in which to carry out essential tasks – is a more pressing problem for women than for men and this is in large part because women still take the major responsibility for child care, the running of the home and shopping and food preparation.

Women who do not have access to a car are able to do less each day and find accessing services such as supermarkets or hospitals more problematic. As we have seen, cars create landscapes of mobility – housing, employment and leisure all built to a low-density pattern with facilities reached only by a vehicle. In many outer estates and low-income neighbourhoods, unless women have access to good social networks they are constrained in what they can do. Typically, a single mother will need family or friends to look after her child while she makes a trip, which may involve two bus journeys, to reach the hospital for an appointment (Grieco 1995). The difficulties are compounded by the fact that on many low-income estates, transport is poor and often slow and unreliable. Grieco writes of inter-household interdependence, strategies to overcome these problems, which she delineates as: (1) provision of shopping services, (2) provision of escort services to members of another household, and (3) provision of child care services (Grieco 1995: 350). Grieco's work was based on a study of time poverty in Merseyside in the early 1990s. Since then, technology has provided some tools which can have the effect of improving connectivity for women in these circumstances. The mobile phone has been a key device to better coordinate lives and arrangements. Likewise, bus companies can now supply real-time information at their bus stops which makes journeys more efficient. But some of the hoped-for improvements for people on low incomes have not been that useful. Teleshopping for groceries is now a widespread phenomenon but most stores charge a standard delivery fee making it less attractive for people on low incomes. Although walking provides excellent aerobic exercise, Bostock's (2001) study of young single parents found that there were many negatives to walking in low-income areas with dependent children. The mothers walked because they could not afford the bus fares and, as Bostock (2001: 15) comments: 'Mothers tried not to think about the poor state of their environment but they could not always escape the sadness of living in a place that had been left to decline.'

Women in transport

Although women drove buses and worked as bus conductors during the Second World War due to men of working age being conscripted, subsequently women have been conspicuously absent from the transport industry. In London only 6 per cent of underground drivers are women and 7 per cent are bus drivers (Transport for London 2004). There is no evidence that the figures for other parts of the UK are very different. Across the transport industry, in bus firms, train companies and taxi firms women are grossly under-represented. They are only 9 per cent of the transport workforce. In addition, there are many jobs which involve driving which are not listed under the heading of transport in occupational categories, for example, driving supermarket delivery lorries, and here too women form a small part of the driving workforce. Women are better represented in the aviation industry, yet study of the figures reveals that they are employed mainly at check-in and as cabin crew rather than as pilots or ground staff (Hamilton et al. 2005: 51). Women are also under-represented at the senior transport policy-making level. In 2007 women made up 42.5 per cent of the Department for Transport's workforce but only 22.8 per cent of senior staff (Department for Transport 2007a).

There is a similar male bias in the transport departments of local authorities and this has been attributed to the fact that transport planners have largely focused on the private car, road building and major engineering projects which meant that few women became interested in transport planning (Little 1994: 147).

Women and public transport

Public transport has a poor image which is not surprising given that, unlike cars, advertising is not promoting buses and trains on our screens nightly. Unfortunately the poor image is a reflection of a reality for many people which puts them off travelling on the bus. Graffiti, dirty buses, smelly waiting areas, drunken, rude and inconsiderate passengers all play their part in making public transport a second-class alternative to the car.

Much can be done to improve vehicles and reduce safety fears. Much has been achieved, as with low floor buses which have greatly helped people with mobility difficulties to get on and off buses, for example. But it is the isolated bus stops and unmanned bus and railway stations which are – certainly after dark – locations where many people will feel at risk of attack. Over the past two decades a number of initiatives have been taken to give travellers a sense of security in order to combat their fears. Closed-circuit television (CCTV) is now a fixture at most rail stations. CCTV is also used on many buses and trains. Many people regret the passing of the bus conductor with the general introduction of one-person operation buses. Equally there is regret at the reduction and removal of staff at railway stations. Waiting at night at the lonely bus stop or the unstaffed railway station can be a fearful experience. A number of stations are unstaffed both day and night, as many as 50 per cent in Scotland (Reid Howie Associates 2000: 101). As the Department for Transport, Local Government and the Regions (2000) advice on gender and public transport puts it: 'A waiting shelter that becomes an attractive venue for young people to meet, or seats that can be lain across by drunks, are not going to provide a secure environment for the lone woman passenger.' A woman waiting at a lonely bus stop at night is a vulnerable target but waiting at a bus station should be a safer experience. Unfortunately the UK's bus stations are not in good shape. When bus services were privatized in the mid-1980s the city or town centre bus stations were often sold off to property developers thus enhancing the bus company's balance sheet. Where this did not happen bus stations were frequently left to decline, with repairs not being carried out, public toilets being locked at night, becoming in some places a magnet for hooliganism and robberies. The drive to accumulate profit led to staff reductions which unfortunately meant that safety was compromised in some areas. As Little (1994: 135) puts it: 'An absence of staff in ticket offices, on platforms and actually on board buses and trains has led to an increase in attacks on women while travelling and in fear of attack.'

Fear of attack is one of the most commonly cited reasons why more women do not use public transport after dark. If they do not have the option of using a car or a taxi then it often means that the trip does not take place, circumscribing their activities. Taxis are an important form of secure transport in these circumstances.

Cars and caring

The ethics of care has been promoted by some feminists as an alternative to a social-justice-based ethical framework. Arguably, both are relevant to a discussion of motoring, gender and the environment. The ethics of care emphasizes the interdependence of individuals, the belief that those particularly vulnerable to our choices require extra consideration and the need to attend to context. Selma Sevenhuijsen (1998: 23) writes: 'Care is, and this cannot be stressed often enough, not only directed at "others" (those in need of care) but also at the self and the physical environment, as well as the interrelations between these.' She goes on to say that we can apply care to the construction of housing by taking into account the needs of those who will live in them. By extension, we can argue that this is as important for street design and for the conduct of drivers on the roads. More so, in fact, because both settings involve many other people, almost all in many settings strangers, and because the threat of death or serious injury is ever present whenever cars are being driven. On the roads all are equal in their cars, part of the speeding flow of traffic, but outside the car are all those who are operating on a different timescale and timetable whether it be the bus passenger or the pedestrian or the cyclist. They lack the metal protection of the car and are more vulnerable.

But caring does not point in one direction. Cars are useful vehicles for keeping in touch with distant family, visiting sick relations, enabling elderly people, whether friends or family, to be given lifts to the shops; and more often than not this work – caring work – is carried out by women.

Men and women, have to make decisions about how best to fulfil their responsibilities, which might entail having regard for the health and well-being of people living in the area when they decide to drive their children to school rather than walk with them. Of course, in reality, these decisions are not so simple, constrained as parents are by the demands of getting to work at a certain time or the perceived or real danger of allowing children to walk to school on their own.

The attachment to the car begins very early in life. It is commonplace for motorist parents to get their small children to sleep by putting them in the car and driving them to sleep. Children from an early age enjoy the sights, the moving panorama, which being a baby passenger gives them. Later in childhood the car is the means by which children are taken to activities – often the school journey is a car journey but so too are the trips to after-school activities. In teenage years parents complain that they have become chauffeurs for their children as they use their cars to transport their offspring to parties and social events. The car then is being seen as part of the caring role of the parent.

The car has another caring role for it is used extensively by a range of 'caring' workers – district nurses, doctors, social workers, occupational therapists – not only to enable them to access their clients in their own homes but also to allow them to transport someone to a hospital appointment or attend a day centre. As the motorization of society produced more and more dispersed communities it became very difficult for these professional staff to carry out their duties without the use of a car.

For more than a decade transport planners in their official documents have been putting those who walk, cycle and use public transport at the top of their transport hierarchy. In practice this does not happen on a daily basis. The reality in most parts of the country is that pedestrians and cyclists are at the bottom of the hierarchy. Streets would be safer if more people were to step out of the self-imposed isolation of the car and mix with others on the street. But the privatized lifestyle of the car encourages us to live apart from others and be fearful of strangers. The 'gated community' is the result of privatized lifestyles made possible by the car.

Men, women and public spaces

To speak of a 'masculine city' as opposed to a 'feminine city' is a useful device to highlight some of the problems with the way in which public space and transport are organized in the contemporary rich world. Petter Naess (2008: 173) explains:

> The 'masculine' city was based on development where women increasingly adopted men's mobility patterns, with the road network and urban land use adapted to steadily growing automobility. The 'feminine' model implied that men, through encouragement and coercion, increasingly adopted women's traditional travelling patterns, with shorter trips and a greater number of trips on foot, by bike and on public transport.

Some feminists argue that the city – its transport systems, land-use patterns, general organization – has been designed by and for men (see Gendersite: www.gendersite.org; Greed 2008). As an illustration of this, Clara Greed highlights the importance of public toilets in moves to get people out of their cars and on to their feet. Her estimate is that there is twice as much public toilet provision for men as for women when it would be fairer if there were more provision for women than men, as women, because of their anatomy, take three times longer than men to use a toilet (Greed 2003: 5). Julia Twigg underlines the importance of this issue: 'Public toilets present issues of citizenship, equality and inclusion, having implications, for example, for the capacity of women and other groups to move about public space' (Twigg 2006: 156).

Clearly, people – both men and women – who value their individual space and security – will take a long time to be persuaded out of their cars. There is a paradox here, however, for unless and until large numbers of people start to walk and cycle then some parts of cities and towns are going to remain unsafe environments.

The car for both male and female motorists is a form of empowerment but it has taken freedom and power away from those who do not drive. As Skeggs has written: 'Mobility and control over mobility both reflect and reinforce power. Mobility is a resource to which not everyone has an equal relationship' (Skeggs cited in Sheller and Urry 2006: 207). There is a persuasive argument made by some sociologists that we need to think of the car driver as a hybrid, and it seems in terms of transport policy that this is one of the most powerful interests around. This is reflected in the way that much car crime, especially speeding, is not treated with the seriousness it deserves. Car-based mobility, like money, is a resource which can be used in all sorts of ways. The next chapter examines the impact of car-based mobility on non-drivers.

Further reading

Redshaw, S. (2008). *In the Company of Cars: Driving as a Social and Cultural Practice*. Aldershot: Ashgate Press. An exploration of the cultural meaning of the car.

Vanderbilt, T. (2008). *Traffic: Why We Drive the Way We Do (And What It Says About Us)*. London: Allen Lane. A fascinating analysis of the human behaviour of motorists.

chapter six

Non-drivers

One could be forgiven for believing that all adults drive a car as this has been an unstated assumption of much transport policy for several decades now. Non-drivers are all those adults who do not have a driving licence. This may be because they are too poor to be able to afford to drive a car, or a non-driver might be someone with a visual impairment or other form of disability which means they cannot pass the driving test. They might be a non-driver because having committed a serious driving offence they have been banned. Or they might have decided to live without a car. Being car free can be an ethical lifestyle choice in a world where carbon emissions from transport contribute significantly to global warming (see www.worldcarfree.net). In a sense, the remaining chapters of this book are also concerned with non-drivers through different stages of the life course.

In this chapter the position of non-drivers is assessed within the contemporary culture of mobility. The Social Exclusion Unit established by the government in 1997 produced an important report on transport and social exclusion in 2003 advising local authorities that they should prioritize accessibility in their transport plans. Much of the policy debate has been around the contribution that poor transport links make to social exclusion, and the government response has been to promote accessibility planning to respond to some of the problems identified. The chapter explores how useful this will be. Finally, we do well to remember that for people living in rural areas transport is extremely important for the maintenance of day-to-day life, and the chapter examines the issues here.

Pooley et al. (2005) have produced a mobility continuum which usefully specifies the various kinds of mobilities. Mobility as movement can be movement around the house or the short walk to the car or, at the other end of the spectrum, it can be international migration. (See Figure 6.1.)

This chapter is concerned with mobility as evidenced in social and

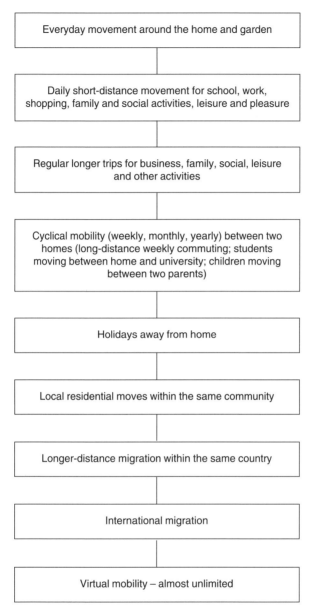

Figure 6.1 Mobility continuum

Source: Pooley et al. 2005: 3

transport policy. There has been a widespread interest in mobilities over the past decade across the social sciences (see Merriman 2007: 1–6; Urry 2007). Much of this work does display a fascination with the novel and the exotic forms of mobility, for example studies of migration around the globe. At the other end of the continuum there is a substantial body of knowledge in health and social care and nursing on the problems affecting those with disabilities and limited mobility. In health and social care, to mobilize means to get someone – usually a frail elderly person – walking again, and mobility is key to the practice of physiotherapy. Keeping mobile is important for the human body, but much of the organization of residential care for older people militates against this. Older people who have walked every day can find within a year or so of moving into residential care that they lose their ability to walk, the reason being that there is no one on the staff available to help them go out for a walk, other residents are perhaps not keen to walk, or staff would prefer that residents stay in their armchairs in the dayroom. Leg muscles not used tend to atrophy and contribute to other health problems.

Social exclusion and transport

In the 1990s a new term, 'social exclusion', entered the poverty debate in the UK. It came from the continental European context, principally France, where socialists had employed the term for some while (Madanipur et al. 1998: 11; Spicker 2007: 65). In Britain, the use of the term by government was a recognition that some families and individuals had not been able to benefit from the rise in prosperity and opportunities that occurred in the previous half century. They had been prevented from participating in many of the activities of daily life enjoyed by the majority of people in the UK.

One of the most persuasive definitions of social exclusion is that it is about participation. 'An individual is socially excluded if he or she does not participate in key activities of the society in which he or she lives' (Burchardt et al. 2002: 30). Burchardt et al. argue that one can break participation down into four categories:

• Consumption: the capacity to purchase goods and services
• Production: the participation in economically or socially valuable activities
• Political engagement: involvement in local or national decision making
• Social interaction: integration with family, friends and community.

(ibid.: 31)

This fourfold delineation of the term 'social exclusion' is helpful when it is applied to transport. Consumption has been greatly affected by an increasingly motorized society in which big retail outlets have been built for car drivers on the edge of cities making them difficult to reach by public transport. Employment has been shifting its location from the central core areas of the city, which was the nineteenth-century pattern, to a much more decentralized configuration in which many people now have jobs in the suburbs and the countryside. These require journeys which can only be undertaken by those with cars. Ways of participating in social life – seeing friends, taking part in voluntary organizations, going to places of entertainment – have become reliant upon the private car, and those who do not have a car, or access to a car, find themselves excluded.

This is captured in this definition of social exclusion by Walker and Walker who write of it as being a 'dynamic process of being shut out, fully or partially, from any of the social, economic, political and cultural systems which determine the social integration of a person in society' (Centre for Transport Studies 2006: 9). This conveys the reality for many people, especially those on low incomes. Their participation in society is limited and partial because facilities are often impossible to reach.

In a world where few people travelled the inability to travel would not matter in the way it does today. The ability to be mobile, to travel to places of employment, leisure or simply to visit friends and family is a necessity of modern life. It was not always so: over a hundred years ago when the study of poverty began with the work of Charles Booth in London in the 1880s and that of Seebohm Rowntree in York in 1899, the people they studied – the urban working class – did not travel far as they were, for the most part, close to their place of work. Most of their life was confined to the place where they lived.

This was a local society where only the very rich had cars so mobility was extremely limited by our standards, although at the time this would not have been judged to be a problem. Pooley et al. (2005: 18) describe the position thus: 'At the end of the nineteenth century most people had very limited choice for their everyday mobility. Most cities were still relatively compact and the majority of everyday journeys were undertaken on foot.' We must not assume that people at the turn of the century wanted to be travelling distances to go to work, shopping or on holiday. (Although Rowntree does note that some of the skilled working class in York did take a few days holiday in Scarborough during August Bank Holiday week (Rowntree 2000 [1901]: 76–7). It could well be that they gained a good deal of satisfaction from the rootedness of their lives and being in one place. So were they socially excluded? Yes, but obviously not because of poor transport links. Booth's East Enders living in poverty and Rowntree's York residents who fell below the poverty line did not participate in society, could not afford to buy a paper, write a letter to absent children (to use examples given by Rowntree) because of a lack of income. In fact it was not until the 1960s that the motorization of British society began to determine where new food shops and places of employment would be situated. The fieldwork for Townsend's (1979) study of poverty in the UK came at the end of that decade.

Mobility, or the lack of it, was increasingly important as the twentieth century progressed. Townsend's definition of disability might equally be seen today as a definition of mobility exclusion. He was writing about the degree to which an impairment or disability prevented them from looking after themselves or running a household. 'Thus disability might best be defined as inability to perform the activities, share in the relationships and play the roles which are customary for people of broadly the same age and sex' (Townsend 1979: 691).

Townsend (1979: 691) grouped activities into those which:

1. Maintain personal existence: includes drinking, eating, sleeping
2. Provide the means to perform these acts: obtaining food, preparing meals, cleaning a home
3. Maintain personal and family relationships
4. Maintain external social relationships: work, in neighbourhood, travelling
5. Are necessary for instrumental roles.

We can map these on to the mobility continuum of Pooley et al. and so find that 1, that is maintaining personal existence, equates with everyday movement while 2 and 4 providing the means is daily short-distance movement. 3 equates with regular longer trips.

For older frail people in the UK the first two on the mobility continuum are all that they manage, but think of a retirement community of British people in another part of the world such as the older British expatriates who live on the Costa del Sol (Betty and Cahill 1999; King et al. 2000; O'Reilly 2000). Their location means that they go from one end of the mobility continuum to the other. The first three points on the mobility continuum are conducted within Spain but holidays, for example coming back to England during the summer months; long-distance commuting and virtual mobility, with email and Skype as the cheapest way to keep in touch with family and friends back in the UK.

It is now conventional to include lack of a car or access to a car as being one of the attributes which can characterize a person as being in poverty (Dorling et al. 2007). The Social Exclusion Unit produced a report on transport and social exclusion in 2003 which highlighted accessibility as a key area in which government departments, local authorities and the public could work together. The report claimed that there was a 'growing recognition' that lack of transport was a significant barrier to social inclusion (Social Exclusion Unit 2003: 1).

The Social Exclusion Task Force took over from the Social Exclusion Unit in 2006 but transport is no longer in its work programme.

Accessibility is concerned with how people reach services, the costs involved, the time involved and safety considerations. However, it is not just about transport but also about how far services are from the population. These are real issues for people without access to a car. The Social

Box 6.1 Five key barriers to accessing services

1. Availability and physical accessibility of transport
2. Cost of transport
3. Services and activities located in inaccessible places
4. Safety and security
5. Travel horizons

Source: Social Exclusion Unit 2003: 2

Exclusion Unit report argued that a principal reason for the decline in mobility for certain groups in society was because no one agency has had the responsibility for seeing that people get to services. This goes to the heart of the problem for it is largely a private service in the UK: buses, trains, taxis and private cars. It is possible to see that local authorities could have the power to take an overall view and to insist that certain estates were not deprived of their bus service after 6 pm or that buses would be run to a particular district on a Sunday. This would mean that there would need to be a rethinking of the concept of public service, a term which is very relevant to transport, for the private sector has an interest in increasing profit whereas the local authority can take the role of representing the public interest. Without an intervention of this kind a significant number of people lose out: they do not make journeys and do not see their friends and family as often as they would like. In a free market society like the UK there are obvious gaps between land-use planning decisions of local authorities concerning where to site facilities, and the decisions of deregulated services such as bus companies who can make up their own minds whether they will run a service. The growing motorization of society means that more people are at risk of not connecting with others if they do not have a car.

We do not know about the number of journeys which are not made by those who are carless. The decentralization of shopping, housing and employment has meant that there are many places that are difficult to access by public transport – it simply does not have the flexibility. The Social Exclusion Unit (2003: 2) gives the example of hospital appointments: 'Over 1.4 million people say they have missed, turned down or chosen not to seek medical help over the last 12 months because of transport problems.'

The definition of transport poverty given in Box 6.2 puts the emphasis on the transport system, highlighting the fact that the poor choices and poor provision of public transport impact negatively on the lives of many people.

Box 6.2 Transport poverty

The cumulative effect of poor public transport services, poor provision for walking and cycling (including access to public transport) and low levels of car ownership, particularly affecting women, the poor, the disabled, dwellers in rural areas and other classically disadvantaged groups.

(Centre for Transport Studies 2006: 17)

Time

We do not know too much about the ways in which social exclusion affects people in everyday life. Not a great deal is known about the amount of time that people spend going about their everyday business if they do not own a car and the extent to which certain journeys are not undertaken because it is felt that they are too time consuming. These are suppressed journeys, journeys not undertaken because they will take too long or because there will be no way of returning the same day. Our lack of knowledge in this area contrasts markedly with the arguments for new roads where time savings for motorists often form part of the case for the scheme. The importance of motorists saving time is part of the dominant car ideology which sees congestion as the number one transport problem, because it holds up movement of goods and people leading to delays in delivering orders, people getting to work on time.

There is also the question of adaptation to low levels of mobility. Gradually, people may well adapt to low levels of mobility, they 'get used to it'. Or people may decide that because of poor transport links they need to move to a better connected part of the country. Church and Frost (2000) believe that time–space organization in households needs exploration: 'the interaction between household members and other individuals (e.g. friends and relatives) and the manner in which time–space budgets influence the ability to travel and travel choices'.

The current government definition of access neglects 'the ability to maintain friendship, family ties and informal connections, the very socialities that organize and structure everyday life' (Cass et al. 2005: 543). Cass et al. draw on the *Poverty and Social Exclusion* report (published in 2000 by the Office for National Statistics), where it is stated that 'almost 14% are too poor to be able to engage in two or more common social activities considered necessary, visiting friends and family, attending weddings and funerals or having celebrations on special occasions' (Cass et al. 2005: 544). The networked nature of family and work relationships means that face-to-face meetings and 'co-presence' are important because of the distances between family members.

Let them learn to drive

The single most important factor regarding getting off unemployment is the ability to drive in order to reach the job (Social Exclusion Unit 2003). Does this mean that government should be subsidizing the cost of driving lessons? The fact that some jobs depend on using a car to reach one's place of work has led some people on low incomes to spend a disproportionate amount of their household budget on a car. This is particularly the case in rural areas where a car is essential not only for getting to work but also for getting to the shops, and often the school.

There will always be those who are too young to drive, too old to drive or too disabled to drive. Do we just ignore their plight? In many ways the fact that this problem was neglected for so long means that this is what has happened. Leaving aside the impact on carbon emissions of many thousands more households and individuals buying cars, it is not always the most efficient way to organize an area's transport system in that many more people can be carried on public transport and at less environmental cost.

Walking, but where to?

If social exclusion is, in part, about the lack of participation, then walking trips remain important for consumption and production, as well as for keeping in touch with friends and family. The most popular transport mode for short journeys for those on low incomes is walking. This is an area where children's needs in the walking environment are greater than those of adults. The quality and safety of these trips has to be safeguarded.

A focus on improving walking conditions and walking environments would benefit not only those on low incomes but the entire community. Residential neighbourhoods which had a 20 mph speed limit in place would be safer for all, not just children.

As can be seen from Table 6.1, the poorest use walking and the bus the most frequently of all the income groups. Their bus use is three times that of the highest income group. They account for approximately one-quarter of all journeys on foot.

But there has to be somewhere to walk to! Unfortunately the number of places convenient to walk to has declined sharply over the past forty years. Post offices have closed, corner shops have gone and, as we have seen, many facilities and shops have relocated to the edges of cities and urban areas. Unless key facilities of this kind are kept within walking distance, motorists drive to these out-of-town locations while the carless are unable to access them. This is a serious restriction on people's quality of life not only because they are unable to reach goods and services which they need but also because

Table 6.1 Use of mode by income quintile: percentage of total trips by mode

| | Income quintile | | | | | |
	Lowest	Second	Third	Fourth	Highest	Total
Walk	24.7	21.4	20.0	17.4	16.6	100
Cycle	18.1	20.8	20.8	19.4	20.8	100
Car	12.0	20.0	21.1	23.5	23.4	100
Bus/coach	32.0	25.7	17.2	14.7	10.3	100
Rail	12.7	11.0	15.3	18.6	42.4	100

Source: Department of Transport 2006a

it weakens social relationships, which are built on face-to-face contact and meetings.

Jane Jacobs in her book *Death and Life of Great American Cities* published more than forty years ago warned of the death of community which accompanied the adjustment to car-borne mobility, the ways in which spatial decentralization made possible by the car leads to many fewer people on the streets who can undertake the informal surveillance which makes those streets safe for children and other vulnerable people, the way in which planned public housing schemes built to improve neighbourhoods end up becoming quite inhospitable and unsafe. Cars are not of course the only cause in this analysis, for particular criticism is made of the planning departments who try to accommodate the car in the city but in so doing destroy some of that which makes people want to live in cities (Jacobs 1962).

What is remarkable about the picture that Jacobs paints of New York City and her particular part of it, Greenwich Village, is the role that shops and shopkeepers play in the community life of an area. They are the local people who are trusted by residents to look after their keys while they are out of town, to take in mail, to act as an adviser. And of course, small shops – and Jacobs is also speaking here of bars and cafés – are important meeting places where small gossip and acknowledgement takes place. These are what another New Yorker has described as 'those great good places' (Oldenburg 1999).

Sad to say then that any discussion of the decline of community and the rise of the car has to take into account the death of the small shop, the corner shop, in the UK. The small shop was part of the community's infrastructure along with the post office and the bank. According to the New Economics Foundation: 'Between 1995 and 2000, the UK lost 20 per cent of some of its most vital institutions: corner shops, grocers, high street banks, post offices and pubs, amounting to a cumulative loss of over 30,000 local economic outlets' (New Economics Foundation n.d.).

Community: access and keeping in touch

When community care was first outlined as a government policy in the early 1960s the impact of the transition to car-based lifestyles was beginning to become apparent. As through the 1960s and into the 1970s the psychiatric and long-stay mental handicap hospitals closed, thousands of people found themselves living in local neighbourhoods. The intention was that their daily contact with people on the street, in the local shops, in the pub would provide them with a much healthier backdrop to daily life. But the powerful trends towards a car-based society has seriously weakened local life.

The ability to reach destinations, to reach out to other people, to walk, to drive, these are all features of living in a community. Those with high mobility capital tend to define what mobility choices will be available for those who are not so well endowed. This is usually a definition or forms part of a definition of independence. According to Willmott and Thomas (1984) there has to be a degree of interaction between people in a community; interests and values need to be shared; local people must feel that they live in an identifiable area and have some kind of attachment to it. This means that much of contemporary British urban and semi-rural and rural space cannot now be so defined. Part of the reason why the car corrodes community is that it is an effective vehicle of lifestyle privatization.

Car dependence is now ingrained and pervasive among social services and health staff. In large parts of the country not to have a driving licence is a bar to field social work. Mobility is an aspiration for so many, so it is unsurprising that recent suggestions from the government's Social Exclusion Unit are that unemployed people learn to drive in order to access the work opportunities that exist. This is the updated version of government minister Norman Tebbit's riposte in the 1980s: when he was told of lack of work in certain areas, he remarked that people in that position should imitate his father who in the inter-war period got on his bicycle in order to look for work.

It would be wrong to think of transport and social exclusion as solely about the provision of services for those who are too old, too young or too poor to drive a car. Certainly, it has to be about improving the coverage, image and popularity of public transport, but it is also about the quality of the society we wish to live in. It can be argued that to have so many people excluded from what the majority of people think of as an acceptable level of participation in work or shopping or social life is detrimental to that society as a whole, that is, to everyone. In health and education we have a basic level of provision delivered through the NHS and the state school system but for transport there is no equivalent basic level of accessibility.

Accessibility planning

One of the major recommendations of the Social Exclusion Unit report was the idea of accessibility planning:

- A clear process and responsibility for identifying groups or areas with accessibility problems.
- In drawing up their Local Transport Plans local authorities have better information on barriers to accessibility.
- Local authorities are expected to work with other local agencies to consider changes in the location and delivery of services.

(Social Exclusion Unit 2003: 62)

As a result, the Department for Transport proposed to local authorities that they include four accessibility indicators in their local transport plans (Box 6.3).

Box 6.3 Accessibility indicators

Education

- Percentage of (a) pupils of compulsory school age, (b) pupils of compulsory school age in receipt of free school meals within 15 and 30 minutes of a primary school and 20 and 40 minutes of a secondary school by public transport.
- Percentage of 16–19-year-olds within 30 and 40 minutes of a further education establishment by pupil transport.

Employment

- Percentage (a) people of working age, (b) people in receipt of job-seekers' allowance within 20 and 40 minutes of work by public transport.

Health care

- Percentage of (a) households, (b) households without access to a car within 30 and 60 minutes of a hospital by public transport.
- Percentage of (a) households, (b) households without access to a car within 15 and 30 minutes of a GP by public transport.

Major shopping centres

- Percentage of (a) households, (b) households without access to a car within 15 and 30 minutes of a major centre by public transport.

Source: Department for Transport 2006a: ch. 7

Social exclusion and transport in rural areas

The low demand for public transport in rural areas illustrates one of the key problems with providing services for those without access to cars. Commercial companies cannot make these routes pay so the cost falls upon local authorities which run them as part of their public service obligation, yet the need for transport services cannot be met entirely by this kind of bus route. Often, demand-responsive services are more appropriate. The passenger telephones and the minibus comes to the door and this would seem to be a useful way to meet some of the transport needs of carless households in rural areas. The transport can be pre-booked to take a person from their home to a particular location – in some areas they are called 'dial a ride'. Clearly these will never match the flexibility or the availability of the private car yet they are more useful than a fixed-route bus, which has an infrequent timetable.

The problems for carless households in rural areas are considerably worse than those of their counterparts in urban Britain. Public transport is poor and often non-existent, which leads many households to buy a car when their low income means that they cannot really afford it. It is striking that carless households in rural Britain make more journeys by car than they do by public transport, revealing the extent to which lifts are given by other people. Needless to say, the problems of carless people have been compounded by the closure of many village shops, post offices and other facilities. Although there are innovative ways around these problems such as 'multi-service outlets', an example of which is a village pub which also sells groceries, they do reveal the countryside's dependence on the car. For many years, rural bus services have been supplemented by community transport schemes – there are now 100,000 minibuses in the UK serving over 10 million passengers each year (Gray et al. 2006: 89). Community transport is a particularly useful service for people who have mobility difficulties through disability, as much of this transport is wheelchair accessible. Yet for disabled people and people over 60 the concessionary bus pass is of limited value in areas where bus services are poor. The Commission for Integrated Transport (2008) has recommended to government that it explore the possibility of integrating taxi's into a demand-responsive system. This would be in 'deep' rural areas with low population density where bus services do not run.

Community care

Discussion of the car is largely absent in social care literature. This is understandable given that much of this literature is about improving care and social work techniques. Yet outside London and a small number of other big cities, social workers would by the 1960s be routinely using cars in order to visit their clients. Not only to visit clients in their homes but also to transport them to day care centres, hospital appointments, to see their relations – all manner of purposes for which a social worker acted as a driver. The car enabled thousands of social workers to live at some distance from the areas in which they worked. This was not uncommon for people in the public sector: it was something that they shared with teachers and other local government staff. The number of social workers who lived in the same area as their clients was probably very small.

Where one might reasonably expect some consideration of the impact of private transport is in the key documents on social work which influenced the education, training and organization of social work in the 1970s and 1980s. The Seebohm Report of 1968 which led to the creation of social services departments in local authorities placed a deal of emphasis on the community, but there was no discussion of the impact of growing mobility for some and reduced mobility for others (Seebohm 1968). The Barclay Report, published in 1982, promoted the idea of community social work, with social workers working closely with the informal networks to be found in an area (Barclay 1982). As with Seebohm, this is not situated in an analysis of the changing nature of neighbourhoods. Even in an appendix on a patch-based model of community social work, there is no discussion of the changes wrought by personal, private mobility.

Community care policies of the 1970s, which involved the closure of long-stay psychiatric and mental handicap hospitals, resulted in provision of hostel accommodation 'in the community'. 'Normalization' of this kind relied on the hostel residents using local services – the doctor, the post office, the shops (Crow and Allan 1994: 171). Thirty years later, in many areas these services have closed and moved elsewhere. This highlights the fact that there is a differential impact as facilities – shops, doctors' surgeries, hospitals – close, with the repercussions ranging from inconvenience for those who have access to a car and can reach services at a distance, to near despair for those, non-drivers, who are literally unable to use the service again. Local authorities and voluntary organizations are often left to pick up the pieces – to put together some form of service whether that be a subsidized bus route, community transport or a supermarket bus.

Conclusion

When community care was first outlined as a government policy in 1960 there were 4.9 million private cars on the road and the impact of the transition to car-based lifestyles was becoming apparent.

Once car ownership by the majority of the population became a reality then real problems emerged. The nature of the relationship between car ownership and the decision to move facilities to out-of-town locations accessible only by cars is complicated as it involves not only planning policy but also the decisions of millions of people. It was, nonetheless, a key moment in the development of UK society, for the individualized society has as one of its central assumptions that we are all motorists. Commonly this is presented, and represented, in our society as a movement to freedom. The ability to determine and decide when and where one wants to go is a unique attribute of the car. There are millions of people who regard this not only as a sign of progress but also as a right with which government – central or local – should not be allowed to interfere.

The forces which led to the social exclusion we have surveyed in this chapter, have transformed the location of industry, shops and services. There is now considerable evidence of the resultant dis-welfares – but there are signs of hope in that the gathering environmental crisis of global warming may well mean that in a more carbon-aware world long distances to work or to shop will be seen as both environmentally and socially regressive. If carbon emissions will have to reduce by 80 per cent by 2050 then much of our carbon-based transport system has to be rethought. This will need to be done so that the accessibility of non-drivers can be improved. Today's children will be middle-aged by the mid-century but it is to their current transport needs that we now turn.

Further reading

Lucas, K. (2004). *Running on Empty: Transport, Social Exclusion and Environmental Justice*. Bristol: Policy Press. A collection of essays on initiatives in both the USA and UK which are attempting to tackle the problem of transport and social exclusion.

Social Exclusion Unit (2003). *Making the Connections: Final Report on Transport and Social Exclusion*. London: The Stationery Office. A document which has set the terms for much of the subsequent debate.

chapter seven

Childhood

> Children want space at all ages . . . Space, that is ample space, is almost
> as much wanted as food and air. To move, to run, to find things out by
> new movement, to feel one's life in every limb, that is the life of early
> childhood.
>
> (Margaret McMillan 1930, cited in Ouvry 2003: 14)

The socialist Margaret McMillan devoted her life to children, first in
Bradford in the 1890s and early 1900s where she campaigned for free
school meals, for school medical inspection and for the improvement of
conditions in general for children. After moving to Deptford in south
London she became a pioneer of nursery education for poor children. Her
concern was improving the lives of slum children who were brought up in
overcrowded, insanitary and unhealthy conditions without sight of green
fields. Children today are materially rich by the standards of a century
ago but her observations on the importance of space and play are still as
relevant.

Today, media discussions of childhood tend to be dominated by stories
of abductions, deaths and cruelty, but over the past decade there has been
a broadening of focus with an increasingly negative commentary on the
state of UK childhood in general. This was highlighted by the publication
of the Unicef report on the quality of children's lives in Europe which
put UK children at the bottom of a league table in 21 industrialized countries (Unicef 2007). Shortly afterwards the Church of England Children's
Society instituted its own inquiry into the state of childhood (Layard
and Dunn 2009). Part of the anxiety about the state of the nation's childhood is to do with the environments in which they are growing up.
The questions which this chapter addresses are: what is wrong with our
local environments and our transport system from the point of view of
children?

Accumulating evidence shows that children's lives are less active than they were, and the resulting decline in physical activity has important and negative consequences for their health. As we shall see, childhood obesity is related to the way in which local areas are designed in our car-dominated society. What do we know about children and transport? How do they get around their neighbourhood? What is the evidence on walking, cycling and children's use of public transport? Why is it that there is so much fear and anxiety among parents which frequently makes them ultra-cautious about letting their children play outside or walk to a friend's house? Finally, we will consider how the evidence we have reviewed and the debates we have considered, relate to social policy for children. But first let us look at the importance of play.

Play: its importance for a child's development

> Play is an essential part of every child's life and vital to processes of human development. It provides the mechanism for children to explore the world around them and the medium through which skills are developed and practised. It is essential for physical, emotional and spiritual growth, intellectual and educational development, and acquiring social and behavioural skills.
>
> (Charter for Children's Play, 1998, quoted in
> Cole-Hamilton et al. 2002)

Play is the way in which a child makes sense of the world. Play can be defined as unstructured activity, that is to say that children make their own play and activities using their imagination and whatever there is to hand: 'Activities which children choose to undertake when not being told what to do' (Cole-Hamilton et al. 2002). From an early age, really from when they first learn to crawl, children want to move, to explore their surroundings and make some sense of them. Play gives children skills which will be useful to them in their adult life. Rogers and Sawyer argue that active involvement in play encourages autonomous thinking, enables children to develop the skill of making sense of their environment and to use the experiences which they have encountered in activity. They list these features of play which help increase cognitive development:

- Play is an active form of learning that unites the mind, body and spirit
- Play provides the opportunity to practise new skills and functions
- Play allows children to consolidate previous learning
- Play allows children to retain their playful attitudes, a learning set which contributes to flexibility in problem solving
- Play develops creative and aesthetic appreciation
- Play enables them to learn about learning – through curiosity, invention, persistence

- Play reduces the pressure or tension that otherwise is associated with having to achieve or needing to learn
- Play provides a minimum of risks and penalties for mistakes.
                    (Rogers and Sawyer 1988 cited in Cole-Hamilton et al. 2002)

The healthy development of children requires that they can engage in play and that they can explore their immediate environment. This is essential for their exploration of their world, as children are engaged in a continuous process of responding and reacting and learning about their surroundings. By the age of 3 years most children will be curious to investigate the wider world outside their home. Recent evidence, however, suggests that not enough children are able to engage with their local environment as they are restricted from outdoors play by the rules of parents and other adults and the diminishing amount of public space. There is some evidence to suggest that children who play regularly in the natural environment demonstrate better coordination, balance and agility (Fjortoft cited in Huby and Bradshaw 2006: 25). It is arguable that this is leading to what has been called 'play deprivation' which is 'a chronic lack of sensory interaction with the world: a form of sensory deprivation' (Hughes in Brown cited in Beunderman et al. 2007).

The car-dependent society is a major cause of this state of affairs and has led to contemporary children spending more time indoors than any other generation of children. This has been helped by the development of computer games and multiple television channels which now absorb much of a child's time. It has recently been estimated that the average child spends 5 hours 20 minutes in front of a screen each day, be that the computer or the television (Ward 2008).

The lost world of the child friendly environment

By definition, children's lives are dependent on those of their parents so that in the period before cars became a majority form of transport – in the 1960s – the opportunities for children to play and explore their locality were much greater. Most housing, in cities and in suburbs, was built before mass car ownership became a reality so did not have garages to accommodate vehicles. To imagine the freedom to play which existed in most towns and cities before the 1960s one only has to imagine a street scene where there were few, if any, cars. As has been amply documented, this was a time when young children were given the permission to travel to school on their own, to run errands and to play in the street (Ward 1978). In the early 1970s, 80 per cent of 7- and 8-year-olds were allowed to go to school on their own. By the 1990s this figure had dropped to only 9 per cent (Hillman et al. 1990).

Once it became a daily mode of transport for the majority of people in the UK car travel transformed social relations. All sorts of changes occurred, often without being noticed or remarked upon. Innumerable daily encounters on the street, between neighbours, or with those with whom one had only a nodding acquaintance, disappeared as walking and cycling were replaced by driving. Fewer people used the streets so that there were fewer people to keep an eye on what was going on. Other social trends reinforced this emptying of the streets, perhaps the most important being the growing employment of women from the 1950s onwards, largely at first in part-time work and then full time. With the advent of the dual-earner family went the loss of another pair of eyes looking out, being in the neighbourhood and being at home.

These environments were not built to be child friendly. After the Second World War the rebuilding of Britain occurred which saw the replanning of cities following war damage and the need to clear slum areas. Too often, walkable and dense neighbourhoods were destroyed in the process. The gains of this rebuilding were obvious – indoor toilets, gardens, good sized houses – while the losses were intangible and not so quickly recognized. It soon became obvious, though, that high-rise flats were unsuitable for families with children, simply because there was no way that parents could keep an eye on their children playing on the ground.

By the 1970s the impact of these changes were being noticed by some observers. Colin Ward, in his book *The Child in the City*, was one notable witness. He wrote: 'Whole areas which were once at the disposal of the explorer on foot are now dedicated to the motorist' (Ward 1978: 118). As Ward pointed out, the car demanded space and this was often the space which previously had belonged to children or anyone else who wanted to use it. Parked cars take up an awful lot of space in the contemporary urban environment. It is much easier to play ball or other games across the street when there are no cars parked at all. Once parked cars begin to intrude then their owners get concerned lest the football hits the vehicle or the car gets scratched, and children are asked to move on and play somewhere else. This began to occur in the late 1950s and early 1960s. Contrast that with the street scene today in most urban and suburban areas in which some cars are parked throughout the day, while in the evenings and at weekends there is continuous parking all along the street. In this street scene, now dominated by the car, children can only really play on the pavement for the road is blocked to them by parked cars; while children and parents alike are terrified of stepping into the road for this now belongs to the car and woe betide the child who questions this. Associated with the rise of the car-dominated neighbourhood has been the proliferation of playgrounds and the installation of play areas in public parks. These are often well used and crowded, but as Colin Ward remarked, children do not require adventure playgrounds in order to play, for they will play in most environments. Indeed, there is a belief that playgrounds are adults' way of keeping children in a 'safe' space, which means that they will not disrupt everyday activities on the street. The famous American writer on urban issues, Jane Jacobs, devoted an entire chapter of her book *The Death and Life of Great American Cities* to the issue of children and streets. Her contention based on her residence in New York City in the 1950s and 1960s was that children wanted to play on the streets, they wanted to be a part of the street scene and as well as playing observe what was going on (Jacobs 1962). Fellow New Yorker Roger Hart was emphatic: 'City children have always wanted to play in the street. . . . All over the world research has shown us that when given the choice children would rather play in the streets than in play grounds. The reasons are simple. Children do not want to be completely segregated from the interesting world of adults' (Hart 1987: 2). One has to say, though, that in many UK cities the busy thoroughfares with small shops and terraced streets leading off them which provided such a varied and ever-changing street scene have been demolished. The houses have been cleared, the shops gone and the main roads replaced by highways which enable traffic to reach into the centre of cities without too much interruption. No responsible adult would want their child to play alongside the new road and no child would be terribly interested in doing so.

Since the 1960s, play has moved indoors, with the outdoors now viewed by many parents and children as hostile, a place where children face the ever-present danger of traffic and the related danger of strangers abducting them. Statistics show that the latter is much magnified by the media, whereas death or injury from cars is a real threat especially, as we shall see, in deprived neighbourhoods. Children's parents are reluctant to allow them to play outside because of traffic or car-assisted abduction and many children are taken to school in the back of a car rather than walking or cycling. The losers here are physical activity and children. According to the *National Travel Survey 2005* only 15 per cent of children aged 5–15 played outside on the street (Department for Transport 2006b).

Valentine (2004: 76–7) calls this the 'retreat from the street'. Imaginative independent play is being lost. Worpole reported that two-thirds of 9–11-year-olds in the UK are dissatisfied with the quality of outdoor play facilities where they live (Worpole cited in Beunderman et al. 2007: 44).

Unfortunately there is a reluctance among adults to change their behaviour so that streets would be safer for children. A glaring example of this was the finding that over half of the adults surveyed would not be prepared to park more than 50 metres away from their house to enable children to play safely and for people to be able to stop and chat (Department for Transport 2004).

Child health

The way we travel has implications for deaths and injuries among children, as well as for their general health via pollution and the erosion of physical activity. Road accidents are the leading cause of deaths in childhood, with motor car accidents accounting for nearly half of all accidental injury fatalities in children (Towner and Dodswell 2001 cited in Millward et al. 2003: 2.3.1). Looking at the incidence of deaths and injuries which are transport-related there is at least a 'good news' story in that child deaths and injuries have declined since the early 1990s.

By 2005 the number of children killed or seriously injured was 49 per cent below the figure for 1994–98. Building on this success the government aims to reduce the annual total of road deaths and serious injuries among children and young people by at least 50 per cent against the 2004–08 average by 2020 (Department for Transport 2009a: para. 37). Given the year-on-year increase in the amount of traffic on the roads this is obviously welcome but it would seem to have been achieved, to some extent, by children disappearing from streets and thoroughfares and by children travelling more inside cars as passengers and reducing the amount of cycling and walking they undertake. Nonetheless the UK has one of the highest child pedestrian fatality rates in western Europe. The rate is twice that of France, Italy, the Netherlands, Sweden, Denmark and Norway. Children in the UK are more exposed to busy roads, wider roads and roads with high traffic levels. The Netherlands, for example, has an extensive network of traffic calmed areas together with properly segregated cycleways. The exposure rates to traffic are the same for UK and Dutch children but Dutch children spend half their pedestrian time in traffic-calmed areas while only 10 per cent of English children do (Bly et al. 1999 cited in Millward et al. 2003: 16).

Road deaths and injuries among children tend to occur in urban areas: in 2005, 74 per cent of deaths and 73 per cent of casualties took place in towns and cities. Eighty-eight per cent of child pedestrian casualties took place that year in urban areas, while for child cyclist casualties it was 83 per cent (Department for Transport 2007b: para. 47).

> In 2005, 28,126 children aged 0–15 were injured in road accidents in Great Britain. 3,331 of these were seriously injured and 141 were killed. These include 11,250 child pedestrian casualties, of which 2,071 were seriously injured and 63 killed.
>
> (Road Safety Strategy 2.11)

Children living in disadvantaged areas are much more likely to be killed or seriously injured by a car. The higher the rate of deprivation the higher the rate of child pedestrian casualties. This has been shown to apply in other countries as well as the UK (Bagley 1992). Among the factors which may explain this are lack of secure play spaces, busy roads and journeys to school which are more dangerous, i.e. might involve crossing heavily trafficked roads. It is also the case that children in disadvantaged areas are more likely to play unsupervised and cross the road by themselves.

The social class gradient was demonstrated when Grayling et al. took all the 71,076 pedestrian casualties in England in 1999 and 2000 and allocated them to the ward in which they occurred. Using the government's deprivation index they were able to show that children in the 10 per cent most deprived wards in England were more than three times as likely to be pedestrian casualties as those in the 10 per cent least deprived wards (Grayling et al. 2002). To add insult to these injuries, children living in the most deprived areas have least access to a car as these wards have the lowest percentage of car ownership. Edwards et al. (2006) found that overall deaths among children in the last two decades of the twentieth century had fallen in England and Wales except in those families where there was no adult in employment. The death rate for injury and poisoning was five times greater for children in the lowest social class than for children in the highest. The overall decline in child deaths they attribute to a reduced exposure risk to traffic whereas for children in social class 5, where motorization is least, there would be relatively more exposure as pedestrians.

Air pollution is another serious impact from road transport on children's health. Children living near busy roads exposed to high levels of particulates – tiny particles of solid or liquid suspended in a gas – are more likely to suffer from respiratory conditions (World Health Organization 2000). There is also evidence that cancers are more prevalent in children who live close to a major source of pollution, which might be a bus station or a busy road. Exposure to high levels of noise, as occurs living on a busy main road, can lead to higher levels of heart disease, insomnia and stress-related conditions. As yet there has not been much work on the impact of road noise on children.

The decline in physical activity

Physical activity starts with crawling and walking and should continue for the rest of life. But as traffic has increased and parental fears have multiplied, children's ability to become physically active has been reduced. Many children lead a much more 'interior' childhood than previous generations, where play is often television or computer assisted. There are real commercial pressures which encourage children to devote inordinate amounts of time to Nintendos, Xboxes and other games. Parents are reluctant to let small children out of their sight given the high levels of traffic and also the fear of abduction. But the nation's health lobby is understandably concerned about the 'couch kids' who spend a sizeable chunk of their day watching television or playing on the computer and not being physically active (British Heart Foundation 2004). Children are introduced early to a culture in which the principal pursuits in leisure time are sleeping, eating and sitting. Sedentary lifestyles are increasingly common in the UK.

The Department of Health recommends, in line with expert opinion, that children should spend an hour a day in physical exercise. But even in education where one might have expected a unanimity on the need for fitness in mind and body there are countervailing pressures. For example, a new city academy in Peterborough was built without a playground because the school wanted children to treat it as a place of work, and besides, playgrounds, it was said, encourage bullies (Hackett 2007).

The government White Paper *Choosing Activity* published in 2005 acknowledged that three out of ten boys and four out of ten girls were insufficiently active. Moreover, 16.6 per cent of boys and 16.7 per cent of girls were obese (Department of Health 2005: 13). The government's response is to coordinate a range of schemes, projects and plans that aim to get children to be more active in their daily lives. Current figures show that 30 per cent of boys and 40 per cent of girls are not achieving the target of an hour of physical exercise each day (Mackett 2001). For children to use their bodies as transport is an excellent way to attain the necessary physical activity. Numerous studies have shown that, certainly in the age group up to 13, children do want to walk and cycle (Brunton et al. 2006). In the past decade, there has been a concentration on the journey to school where local authorities and central government have tried hard, through a variety of 'safe routes to schools' schemes, to popularize walking and cycling to school rather than depending on the car. Despite these efforts the proportion of journeys to school by car is increasing. 'Between 1992–1994 and 2002–2004, trips to primary school by car increased by 11 per cent and by foot reduced by 11 per cent' (National Travel Survey cited in Smith et al. 2006: 19).

It would appear that walking to school can improve the mental health of children as well. For example, the World Health Organization (2004a: 38) report that walking to school rather than being brought by car meant that children

• Obtained a lower score on a depression index
• Had a lower score in aggression/hostility
• Had a lower score on an anxiety measure.

Education trips account for only one-third of trips made by children and these trips are shorter than others by children (Mackett 2001). Inevitably, the full range of children's journeys need to be examined to increase our understanding of them. Using data from the National Travel Survey, comparing figures from 1985/86 to 1997/99, Mackett concludes that children are making fewer trips, but when they do travel they go further distances and make more use of cars (Mackett 2001).

Walking is the ideal aerobic exercise, but sadly children are walking less. Because parents are so reluctant to allow their children to go out on their own up to the age of 10 or 11, the patterns of walking for adults bear directly on the transport choices of children insofar as most children of primary school age will be escorted by an adult on their journeys. Before the age of 10 most child journeys are made with parents, and children are mainly car passengers for these journeys. From the National Travel Survey we can see that the average distance walked decreased by 20 per cent in the 1990s (Department for Transport 2005b: 1). Reasons given by children in recent research for the negative image of walking include:

- Walking is too slow
- Children fear the traffic
- Stranger danger
- Fear of bullying
- Weather
- Embarrassment of walking with parents.

(Smith et al. 2006: 12)

After the age of 11, when children want to be independently mobile, cycling and walking could become important for them. Unfortunately, 'the last two or three decades have seen a dramatic fall in the distance cycled by children and young people under 16 years of age: around 40 per cent for boys and over 50 per cent for girls' (Gill 2005: 4).

Children are increasingly found to be overweight, and childhood obesity is a growing problem characterized by a weight well above the mean for a child's height and age and a body mass index well above the norm.

Obesity in children has been classed by the World Health Organization as an epidemic. In 2001 at least 10 per cent of Scottish children aged 4–5 were classified as obese while 20 per cent of Scottish 11–12-year-olds were deemed to be obese (Reilly et al. 2006). The pathway to obesity begins with a physically inactive way of life before children go to school.

In addition to the growth in childhood obesity other health effects are early onset of type 2 diabetes, increased risk of heart disease in later life and osteoporosis. High levels of traffic and unsafe public space contribute to 'obesogenic environments', that is to say those factors which play a part in determining both nutrition and physical activity (Jones et al. 2007: 12).

Risk and fear

In December 2007 the *Guardian* newspaper carried this item in its Family section. Lisa Bacon (a pseudonym) wrote:

Thursday, 1 pm, about to have lunch. Knock at the door. It's a woman from children's services come to investigate an anonymous report made about me to the National Society for the Prevention of Cruelty to Children (NSPCC). Was it true, she asked, that I let my seven-year-old son walk to and from school alone . . .? Seven weeks earlier, I had started letting my son (who's now eight) travel 1 km each way to and from school alone. We live in a quiet residential area and almost the only cars on the road are those on the school run. We discussed where was safe to cross and I followed behind as I have another school age child, so I always knew my son got to school OK. After school we met before he headed off. . . .

(Bacon 2007)

What is remarkable about this story is not only that the NSPCC should be contacted by other parents but that the boy was not really walking to school on his own but being escorted – at a distance – by his mother. Above all, it reveals the extent of the fear in our society around the issue of allowing children to walk on their own. The dominant theme in discussions of cycling and walking to school or cycling and walking by children in general is that they should defer to the dangers from road traffic, cross safely, wear reflective clothing, travel with other people etc. etc. This is all good advice but far less attention is paid to the road danger caused by traffic. As Gill has written:

the more obvious threats to children's safety – notably those from road traffic – are not treated with anything like the same degree of obsessive control as that applied to other areas where children congregate. Car travel, it appears, is so essential and important to easing our lives that we are not prepared to apply so much rigour to the ensuing risks.

(Gill 2007: 77)

Gill identifies four kinds of arguments about risk. The first is that children need some kind of involvement with risk in order to manage the risk. This would apply to learning to cycle or swim. The successful negotiation of risk leads to a growth in confidence in the child. The second is that many children have an appetite for risk which needs to be satiated, hence such things as skateboard parks. This might be termed risky behaviour and it is obviously not what is wanted on the road environment however much children might see their parents engage in it with dangerous driving. The third argument around risk is that children gain benefits from undertaking risky tasks and these might be health or developmental. Kegerreis (1993) argued that children need to make the school – and presumably other – journeys on their own because this enabled them to mature, to make decisions about risk and danger for themselves and in so doing gain in confidence. Finally, risky situations are seen as character building (Gill 2007: 15–16).

In 1993 John Adams, a co-author of the pioneering study *One False Move* – which demonstrated how children were losing the freedom to travel to school on their own at ages 7 and 8 – argued that there were two options given the danger from traffic: either remove the danger from children or remove the children from the danger (Adams 1993; Hillman et al. 1990). It is the latter which has occurred with walking and cycling rates in decline among children. Escorting of children to and from school has become a major activity for parents of primary age children. Here again there are healthy ways to escort, either walking or cycling to school with a child or driving him or her which is normally, and erroneously, called 'the school run'. A great deal of the fear of parents around the risk to their children's lives from traffic would be reduced if the UK were to invest substantial sums in traffic calming with speed limit enforcement and properly segregated cycleways. As we have seen there is ample evidence that unless this is done then levels of physical activity by children will continue to decline. Home Zones are an example of the kinds of measures which are required.

Home Zones

Home Zones are areas which have been designed so that traffic does not take priority and the streets within them are seen not just as thoroughfares for traffic but also as social space where people can meet, chat and children can play. Usually this means that the maximum speed is 20 mph but often it is set at 10 mph. Traffic is forced to travel slowly by the use of humps in the road, removing the distinction between the road and the pavement and by adding trees and plants. There are now upwards of a hundred Home Zones in the UK although this country lags far behind the Netherlands and Germany where there are thousands and their introduction dates back more than twenty years. Home Zones are designed to give more of a sense of place, to make the area more attractive and provide a safer space in which children can play. In an evaluation of the Home Zones, Webster et al. found that the most popular activities for children after the Home Zone was created were: chatting, football, riding bikes or scooters, chasing games and hide and seek, in that order (Webster et al. 2006: 68). To create a Home Zone is not cheap for a local authority as it means substantial modifications to the road layout and design in 'retro-fitting' an area. Nonetheless the Zones represent a positive approach to the fact of increasing traffic and diminishing opportunities for children to play and meet their friends.

Transport policy for children

The issues we have reviewed in this chapter are, like most policy problems today, resolvable by a combination of changes in individual behaviour and structural changes by government. It would be foolish to ignore the many changes for the good which can come from changes in individual behaviour and there is emerging evidence that social marketing campaigns are able to effect some changes in travel behaviour and choices (Sloman 2006: 53–4).

Worcester is one of the Sustainable Travel Demonstration Towns and in one part of the city in the first 12–18 months public transport trips increased by 14 per cent, walking by 17 per cent and cycling by 32 per cent while car trips reduced by 12 per cent (Metz 2008: 89). But these need to be accompanied by changes in the local environment which will overwhelmingly benefit the needs of children. Foremost among these has to be the reduction in danger from moving traffic which we know from foreign examples can be achieved by financing a large programme of Home Zones together with a reduction in the speed limit to 20 mph in residential areas. As we have seen, not only would this enable children, and adults as well, to walk and cycle but it would also enable children to play on the streets of the Home Zone, while a general 20 mph limit would make it safer for children to make their way to the park or playground.

There needs to be an acknowledgement that the risk from traffic is being borne disproportionately by children who live in deprived areas where car ownership rates are low. 'Children in low income families are less likely to have access to a car as a mode of travel. The Department for Transport's National Travel Survey reported that 54 per cent of households in the lowest income quintile had no car compared with eight per cent in the highest. Over half the households in the highest quintile had two or more cars' (Smith et al. 2006).

The present government has headlined the need for children to be more than passive spectators when changes are envisaged for their area. Instead, the government believes that they should become participants and their views listened to with care. This perspective is at the core of the Children's Plan released in 2007 by the Department for Children, Schools and Families (2007). The issue of play is highlighted at the beginning of this document and extra money is to go into creating and renewing playgrounds for children, with local authorities being encouraged to create more 20 mph areas and Home Zones as part of this strategy for play (Department for Children, Schools and Families 2008). However, as we have noted, the rising volumes of traffic, the decline in levels of physical activity and the rise in obesity are formidable problems and it may well be that these measures, although pointing in the right direction, are insufficient to deal with the size of the task. If these measures are to be introduced in the context of rising traffic volumes then the problem of unsafe areas persists. In some residential areas the closing of some roads to traffic could enable them to 'be returned to communities for recreation and green space' (Sustainable Development Commission 2007: 40). Further, we know that more than half the driving population regularly ignores the 30 mph limit so there is a question, involving police manpower and resources, as to how the new 20 mph limits will be enforced. In sum, a transport policy for children, based on healthy and environmentally benign principles would make car travel much less attractive and walking and cycling much more attractive.

Children's needs in transport policy were neglected for decades as children were just one part of the non-driving population of this country who became 'immobilized others' (Thomsen 2004). Social policy for children centred on children's services throughout the post-war period. Even the discovery of 'children's rights' from the 1970s – part of a general fashion for rights language in social policy as in 'welfare rights' – ignored the way in which their right to play in the local environment had been effectively withdrawn. This was highlighted when article 31 of the 1989 UN Convention on the Rights of the Child included a child's right to play and this was ratified by the UK government two years later.

Moss and Petrie argue that social policy for children has now to have an emphasis on supporting and creating spaces where children meet and engage with one another. These would be places where children can be themselves away from the 'adult gaze' (Moss and Petrie 2002: 107). The 'adult gaze' is an accurate description of the loss of independence in childhood which has resulted, in part, from the hegemony of the car. Many children from an early age are strapped in the back of their parents' car, taken to nursery, then school, holidays, after-school activities. There can be no denying the wealth of experience that car ownership brings for children. At the same time we have to constantly bear in mind the accompanying loss of freedom for all children and the loss of so many opportunities for children from carless families. In fact, there is a mounting body of evidence which suggests that a childhood which is so interconnected with the lives of adults postpones maturity and responsibility in children. The 'commodification of childhood' is a part of this adult surveillance – the nursery school sector, the leisure businesses which cater for children, the electronic and media industries. Moreover, and, as we have seen, this has in some part led to the growth of a sedentary lifestyle for our children with a worrying drop in physical activity.

Further reading

Beunderman, J., Hannon, C. and Bradwell, P. (2007). *Seen and Heard: Reclaiming the Public Realm with Children and Young People*. London: Demos.
Layard, R. and Dunn, J. (2009). *A Good Childhood: Searching for Values in a Competitive Age*. London: Penguin.

Disability

If driving licences were distributed on the basis of need then disabled people unable to walk would be first to receive them. The great majority of drivers in our society are able bodied – and perfectly well able to walk and to cycle – so would not have a strong claim to a licence. Yet, as we know, this is not how the car system works as it bestows greater mobility on the most active adults while often, in fact, increasing the mobility problems of disabled people. The car is a technology which has come to define our society and in so doing has dis-abled some people while extending freedom and opportunities to others. This chapter explores this ambivalence in the area of disability. The legislative context for disability policy has been strengthened by the Disability Discrimination Act 1995. The definition of a disabled person under the Act is someone who 'has a physical or mental impairment which has a substantial and long-term effect on his ability to carry out normal day-to-day activities'. Transport is about the everyday comings and goings in people's lives and this chapter examines the extent to which the transport environment is accessible to disabled people and the degree to which it still discriminates against them.

In the first part I will examine the relationship between the car system and disability and then look at the ways in which disabled people get around and the problems they encounter particularly in relation to public space. Road traffic crashes are responsible for a considerable amount of death and serious injury and the dimensions of this problem are explored. Government has responded to the mobility difficulties of some disabled people through the benefits system, and the nature and extent of this assistance is outlined. Finally, given that government is committed to a society where disabled people are socially included, what would an inclusive transport system look like?

Disability and the car system

We are encouraged to think of transport as machines for mobility by the car system. Walking is an important form of transport too and to lose the ability to walk is to be deprived of an important freedom, to move around the house, to get to local services and facilities, in effect, to be disabled.

Equally, cycling is an individual form of transport which enables door-to-door journeys of some distance to be undertaken. The car has eclipsed these alternatives for personal transport and relegated public transport to the status of second best. The car system disables those with impairments in a way which would not have occurred in the past or in some other societies in the present. For example, in a country in which public transport was the dominant mode of transport used on a daily basis by millions of people the fact that one did not possess a driving licence would not be significant as most facilities – shops, places of entertainment, employment – would be accessible by public transport. Indeed, there are still some places in the world where cars have not become the dominant transport mode.

The social model of disability contends that society disables people with impairments – an impairment is a limitation caused by physical or sensory problems – through the construction of social and economic barriers (Barnes and Mercer 2003). These barriers can mean that a disabled person has a significantly reduced quality of life compared with a non-disabled person. The car system is a good illustration of this. If one does not possess a driving licence then meetings, social life and employment, outside of major urban areas with excellent public transport, are all made more difficult. Many jobs now require the ability to drive and the Social Exclusion Unit report on transport showed a clear association between driving and finding employment for people in deprived areas (Social Exclusion Unit 2003). Campion et al. (2003) found that about half the disabled people in their survey had turned down a job offer or interview because of the absence of accessible transport. Sixty per cent of disabled people in the UK did not have household car access in 2002 (DPTAC 2002). This figure increased to 62 per cent for wheelchair users and 88 per cent for those with a visual impairment (Campion et al. 2003: 9–10). The high unemployment rate among disabled people is a partial reflection of this. According to the Labour Force Survey, nearly one in five people of working age (6.9 million, or 19 per cent) in Great Britain are disabled and only half of disabled people of working age are in work compared with 80 per cent of non-disabled people of working age (Legge et al. 2006).

Since the end of the Second World War space has been designed for the benefit of car-based lifestyles. Cities have been rebuilt in order to cope with traffic and its demands which comprise not only roads but large areas to be set aside for car parking. As Freund (2001: 696) has observed: 'Spatial social organisation is not neutral, but rather political in the priority it gives some transport modalities and in the way it "handicaps" others.' The police, who are concerned with the enforcement of traffic law, invariably give precedence to the rights of traffic. Traffic flow is important to the police so that cars parked illegally on the pavements are not dealt with harshly as they do not obstruct the flow of traffic. The fact that they obstruct the path of pedestrians seems to be much less important, as is the fact that for some disabled people a car or van parked on the pavement may prevent them passing at all. High traffic levels induce fear in pedestrians – particularly when they have to cross heavily trafficked roads – but disabled people can feel themselves much more vulnerable, and whether they use a wheelchair, a walking aid or a guide dog they do not possess the dexterity which is required of the modern city dweller in public spaces.

Sometimes the aids that disabled people use to navigate their way along the pavement identify them as easy targets for mugging or verbal and physical abuse. A recent study claimed that 60 per cent of blind and partially sighted people have been a victim of verbal and/or physical abuse (Action for Blind People 2008: 5).

Freund comments that speed rules transport spaces and public spaces in general. This makes movement more difficult: 'Poor pedestrian signals, short traffic lights, the designs of transport platforms (e.g. roadways) materialise an organisation of space–time that favours the "quick" and the "spry", and disables those who are not' (Freund 2001: 697). This can lead to serious consequences for disabled people as they may not attempt to compete with the hostility that they feel towards them from the organization of the transport environment. It means that they are more likely to stay out of public spaces and, like children, inhabit private space most of the time. This increases physical inactivity, which can lead to other medical problems (Aldred and Woodcock 2008: 491). On the other hand, one must remember that there are impairments which permit some disabled people to drive cars and enjoy the mobility, freedom and opportunities which this allows. Twenty per cent of disabled people drive (DPTAC 2002). For these disabled drivers the car is a lifeline connecting them to the wider world.

Similarly the opportunities open to disabled people who drive are greater than for those who do not: employment being a key area. Cars bestow upon their users a freedom – a freedom to go when and where they like, and to be without that freedom when one has enjoyed it all one's adult life is a deprivation. Davey quotes a respondent, who had been forced to give up driving because of age and infirmity, as saying: 'It has made me a total prisoner in here . . . I can't go out and I can't do anything' (Davey 2007: 54). People who are disabled in mid-life – sometimes as the result of a car crash – suffer the same loss although in the case of a crash it is sudden and no time is available to prepare for this.

That public spaces, pavements and roads are not built with the needs of disabled people in mind should not surprise us, for city planning and design since the Second World War has emphasized mobility (Imrie 1998: 130). Countless cities were rebuilt to allow fast access to their centres from the suburbs and from motorways in the belief that this would ensure economic development and prosperity. To this end wholesale demolition of existing communities destroyed local shopping centres close to where people lived.

Because the car system is now so dominant in all our lives other forms of transport have had to adapt to its power. Bicycles preceded cars in the history of transport but have had to submit to the car. Because of the dangerous nature of the road for cyclists and in the absence of properly segregated cycle paths many cyclists choose to cycle on the pavements instead of the road. For those people with disabilities who walk this is a source of some anxiety as they feel threatened by cyclists who cycle on pavements. Thus the risk and the fear have been transferred to the more vulnerable travellers, from motorists to cyclists to pedestrians.

As we have seen in earlier chapters the rise of the mass car society has changed the geographical distribution of housing, employment, shops and public services. We no longer only have suburb to city centre commuting for work but suburb to suburb commutes and what the Americans call 'reverse commutes', city centre to suburb. Public transport does not have the flexibility to replicate all these journeys and this adds to the pressure to use the car. The city or town centre with facilities and shops reasonably close together and easily accessible by public transport has lost many of these to a range of suburban and even semi-rural locations – often chosen because they are convenient for parking and close to major roads – putting those with disabilities and those who cannot drive at a serious disadvantage.

Sometimes when there is public transport the journey is so time consuming with more than one change that it not worth the time taken. This leads to 'trip inhibition' among non-drivers where they do not consider a journey because of the time and trouble it would take. For many disabled people it is not simply the wearing nature of waiting at bus stops for buses which are late or do not turn up at all but also the disability itself which makes a journey difficult or hazardous. Getting on and off the bus, not being able to see the number of the bus when it arrives at the stop, being thrown to the floor when the bus driver does not wait for a person to sit down before the bus moves off from the stop are just some of the difficulties encountered. Unfortunately, in a number of surveys there is consistent criticism of bus drivers and other public transport staff for their negative attitudes to disabled people (DPTAC 2002; Campion et al. 2003; Wilson 2003: Webster and Shah 2008).

The car offers safe and secure environments for people to travel door to door. It elevates private space while at the same time weakening public space. Consumer societies are structured around the presupposition that we are all freely choosing individual and privatized consumers/drivers. Once because of age, infirmity, disability or poverty one moves outside the car system then life is more problematic and one's ability to participate and to travel is much more constrained. It is understandable that in a car-dependent society so many want to keep their driving licence for as long as possible but it remains a private solution to the problem of car-dominated public space.

Public space

> Public space relates to all those parts of the built and natural environment where the public has free access. It encompasses all the streets, squares and other rights of way, whether predominantly in residential, commercial or community/civic uses; the open spaces and parks; and the 'public/private' spaces where public access is unrestricted (at least during daylight hours). It includes the interfaces with key internal and external and private spaces to which the public normally has free access.
> (Office of the Deputy Prime Minister 2004: 10)

A great deal of attention has been paid to public space in recent years by government, quangos, voluntary organizations and pressure groups. For years public space was treated as merely the space between buildings which could look after itself. This has changed as more and more incursions on public space have emerged and the car system has not only emptied streets of people but also made some areas quite dangerous. For the pedestrian, pavements have become more hazardous with advertising A-boards, wheelie bins, bollards and other street furniture on the increase. Bollards, in particular have multiplied to prevent cars parking on pavements but reducing the width of the walkway and presenting a hazard for visually impaired people.

The difficulties experienced by disabled people in public space are determined by the nature of their disability. Wheelchair users need sufficiently wide pavements for safe passage. Blind and partially sighted people require an absolute minimum of obstructions on the pavement. For them, cars parked on the pavement and broken and cracked paving stones are all hazards which could injure them. As we shall see in the next chapter, falls are a major cause of injury. Walking journeys would be improved by more provision of accessible public toilets and better public toilets. Even in city centres these can be scarce and this leads to disabled people thinking twice about making a shopping journey, for example. A study of Leeds city centre commented: 'Even where there are claims of accessible toilets, there can still be steps to the toilets, toilet cubicles can be too small to manoeuvre in a wheelchair, handles or knobs can be too high or difficult to turn, and toilets can be too high to reach' (Barrett et al. 2003: 236).

The desire to improve the urban environment in the UK has led to some interest among planners in what has been achieved in some other European cities. Copenhagen has been of especial interest as the city centre has over the past four decades been progressively redesigned to give precedence to pedestrians, with major restrictions on car parking. The ideas of Jan Gehl have been central to this and he has advised a number of UK local authorities. This has restored safety and sociability and not only enabled a more relaxed city life but also shown how walking can contribute to a revivified city (Gehl 2001).

Linked to this has been the idea of shared space which removes physical barriers such as kerbs, road signs, edge of pavement barriers in an effort to get us to think of streets as places rather than as solely conduits for traffic. The net effect is to reduce traffic speed and to give more confidence to other road users to walk, chat, shop and congregate. This entails relying on motorists to respond to the visual clues from pedestrians and vice versa as to where they are going, and so presents major problems for some disabled people, particularly those who are blind or partially sighted. It may be that some 'safe space' can be created within shared space to protect them. This illustrates that creating an inclusive environment is not straightforward as many people's interests have to be taken into account.

Disability created by the car system

The World Health Organization estimates that each year between 20 million and 50 million people are injured or disabled because of road traffic crashes. The wide range is because of the under-reporting of such incidents (World Health Organization 2004b: 5).

The psychological and social consequences of road crashes can be considerable both for the victims and for their families. Some of the disabilities created are personality changing. Motor vehicle crashes are the leading cause of traumatic brain injury (World Health Organization 2004b: 48). With certain kinds of traumatic brain injury the person one knew and loved might have disappeared and one has to get to know a new person who will probably be highly dependent.

In the EU more than 50,000 people a year are killed on the roads and more than 150,000 are disabled for life by road crashes (World Health Organization 2004b: 50). A European study of the impact of road crashes on victims and their families found that 90 per cent of the families of those killed and 85 per cent of the families of disabled people reported 'a significant permanent decline in their quality of life'. The victims and their families experienced nightmares, headaches, sleeping difficulties and general health problems.

Road deaths and serious injuries have been falling for more than a decade and this can be counted a public health success story. Yet despite this, approximately eight people a day die on UK roads. Figures for deaths and serious injuries have been in decline but this is because of reduction in exposure of cyclists and pedestrians – the most vulnerable road users – to

Table 8.1 The 20 leading non-fatal injuries sustained as a result of road traffic collisions, world, 2002

Type of injury sustained	Rate per 100,000 population	Proportion of all traffic injuries %
Traumatic brain injury (short term)	85.3	24.6
Open wound	35.6	10.3
Fractured patella, tibia or fibula	26.9	7.8
Fractured femur (short term)	26.1	7.5
Internal injuries	21.9	6.3
Fractured ulna or radius	19.2	5.5
Fractured clavicle, scapula or humerus	16.7	4.8
Fractured facial bones	11.4	3.3
Fractured rib or sternum	11.1	3.2
Fractured ankle	10.8	3.1
Fractured vertebral column	9.4	2.7
Fractured pelvis	8.8	2.6
Sprains	8.3	2.4
Fractured skull (short term)	7.9	2.3
Fractured foot bones	7.2	2.1
Fractured hand bones	6.8	2.0
Spinal cord injury (long term)	4.9	1.4
Fractured femur (long term)	4.3	1.3
Traumatic brain injury (long term)	4.3	1.2
Other dislocation	3.4	1.0

Note: Short term means a matter of weeks whereas long term is until death, with some complications resulting in reduced life expectancy.

Source: World Health Organization 2004b

road traffic as is seen in the reduction in both activities. Road crashes, however, remain the leading cause of death and disability for those aged under 40.

The government's road safety strategy aims to make substantial reductions in the figures for those killed and seriously injured, yet this is a difficult task when around 1 million extra vehicles come on to the roads each year.

Public transport

Buses

When it comes to public transport the disabled population, like the general population, make much more use of buses than of trains.

Disabled people in England and Wales use buses 20 per cent more frequently than non-disabled people but only 42 per cent of disabled people are satisfied with their local bus services (DPTAC 2002).

Public transport, like towns and cities, was not designed with disabled people in mind so there has been a process of redesigning and refitting to comply with disability legislation. By 2017 all buses must be accessible for disabled people which means that they must have low floor entry, have space to accommodate a wheelchair and have bright visible markings. These changes in bus design have benefited other people as well – parents with pushchairs now do not have to collapse their buggies before boarding the bus but can walk straight on with them.

The change to one-person-operated buses meant the end of the conductor in most parts of the country. Conductors were valued by some people as they could help passengers who had mobility difficulties and had a role in restraining bad behaviour on the bus. Although the Mayor of London has announced his intention to bring back conductors on certain routes it is doubtful that this would be a policy adopted nationwide given the additional costs involved.

Although the redesign of buses to make them disabled person friendly is greatly to be welcomed, it is worth bearing in mind the fact that disabled people who have difficulty walking up to a quarter of a mile find problems in reaching bus stops (Gallon cited in Wilson 2003: 30).

Bus stops themselves are often a problem for disabled people because of obstacles at the stop and cars illegally parked which make it impossible for the bus to draw up close to the kerb. Bus stops in a state of disrepair can also be a significant hazard for some disabled people (Webster and Shah 2008: 14).

Buses have an important role in the provision of transport for disabled people but they lack the flexibility of other forms of transport.

Trains

Disabled travellers find trains to be the most inconvenient and difficult to use of all the transport modes (DPTAC 2002). Only 20 per cent of those surveyed by DPTAC were satisfied with local trains and only 12 per cent with long-distance trains. DPTAC found that two-thirds of its sample never used local trains while three-quarters never used long-distance trains.

Taxis

In rural areas in particular, buses play a minor role in the transport of people. For a disabled person living in the countryside, taxis are a favoured form of transport affording them the door-to-door convenience enjoyed by car drivers and passengers. But the costs of using taxis on a regular basis are high notwithstanding the payment of the mobility component of the Disability Living Allowance.

A number of local authorities have responded to the high costs of taxis by introducing a taxi card scheme. Under this scheme people who have serious mobility problems are able to pay a flat rate for their journey while the rest of the cost is paid for by their local authority. Those who are eligible for a taxi card are people who receive the higher rate mobility component of the Disability Living Allowance, people who are registered as blind and those who are in receipt of a War Pension Mobility Supplement. The London scheme is the most generous with some London boroughs subsidizing the cost of over 100 taxi journeys a year. At present, 42 of the 150 local authorities in the UK use a voucher scheme (DPTAC 2002). As taxis are such an important form of transport for disabled people it is to be welcomed that all of them will be wheelchair accessible by 2010.

Most parts of the UK have a community transport scheme which provides door-to-door travel – usually in wheelchair-accessible vehicles – often using a 'dial a ride' service. Naturally these play a particularly important role in semi-rural and rural areas where conventional bus services are at best patchy and at worst non-existent.

Mobility benefits

Concessionary fare schemes for disabled people on buses have been in existence for some years but have differed according to the local authority area. Usually, concessionary fares for disabled people have been offered on the same basis as those for older – 60+ – people. But some authorities were more generous than others and some were more flexible. There were variations between authorities as to the start time – in some places the concession started at 9 am while in others it was 9.30 am. Disabled and older people living in London have had free travel during the day for many years while in some local authority areas there was no scheme and in others the concession was half-price travel. Some uniformity was introduced by the Transport Act 2000 which required all local authorities in England to provide at least half-fare travel for people over 60 and for disabled people. The concessionary fare pass is held by 48 per cent of disabled people (DPTAC 2002). The next major extension of this scheme was in 2008 when all local authorities were subsidized by the government to introduce a national concessionary scheme which gave free travel throughout the length and breadth of England. This meant that a person could use their pass anywhere in the country. Previously the pass had only been valid in their local authority area or in adjacent local authorities. Scotland and Wales had introduced free travel on buses in 2002.

Some fifty or so local authorities – the biggest of which was Portsmouth – had offered more flexibility. Bearing in mind that many disabled people cannot use buses as they may not be able to walk to the bus stop or have mobility difficulties which prevent them from boarding a bus, they offered tokens which could be used to pay for taxi fares as an alternative to the travel card. Help the Aged working with Portsmouth City Council surveyed more than 12,000 of those who applied for the concession and found that 48 per cent had opted for tokens as against 52 per cent for the bus pass (Help the Aged 2007). Nevertheless, there remain important questions about the concessionary fare schemes. Are they the best use of money to help those with mobility difficulties for there may be many people getting free travel who could afford to pay the fare. Similarly, would it not be more appropriate to offer tokens to all those over 60 or who are disabled?

The Disability Living Allowance is a tax-free non-means-tested benefit for adults and children with disabilities who either need help with looking after themselves – the care component – or who find it difficult to get around – the mobility component. The latter is paid at two rates. The higher rate of the mobility component is to provide financial assistance to those who need to use taxis because their disability prevents them from walking, while the lower rate is paid to those who can walk but their disability means that most of the time they need help and guidance from others.

Forty per cent of disabled people have a car in their household and, of these, 69 per cent hold a blue badge. The blue badge scheme provides a range of parking concessions for people with severe mobility problems who have difficulty using public transport. Cars displaying the badge can make free use of parking meters and other concessions. Approximately two-thirds of badge holders are over the age of 65 and 55 per cent do not use public transport (Department for Transport 2008b: 7).

Motability was established in 1977 to enable disabled people to obtain a car using their Mobility Allowance. It only applies to those receiving the higher rate mobility component of the Disability Living Allowance and the disabled person does not have to drive the car but can own it and it can be driven by someone else for them. Seven per cent of all cars purchased in the UK are bought using Motability (DPTAC 2002). The scheme also applies to mobility scooters. Most customers simply transfer their mobility component to Motability and then have the use of a car for three years. Models are changed every three years.

Mobility scooters are extremely useful for those people who, for whatever reason, are unable to walk very far. There are two kinds: one which has a maximum speed of 4 mph and is designed for use on the pavement and another which has a maximum speed of 8 mph and is for use on the road.

An inclusive transport system

The progress made towards a more inclusive transport system must not be discounted. Accessible buses, taxis and trains are in service and coming into service and have already improved the transport opportunities for many people. Similarly, the national bus pass is an important benefit for many disabled people who can use buses. In these ways transport disability, 'the unnecessary exclusion of disabled people from current forms of transport' (Heiser in Zarb 1995), is being tackled.

A good deal can be done by improving the machinery of transport, but human behaviour in public space is much more difficult to change. There is some evidence that the attitudes of public transport staff need to improve. Hostility and violence towards disabled people must be a real concern and require a considered response from the police, legal system and education. Quite possibly we are reaping the legacy of the invisibility of so many disabled people in the past which led to attitudes that they should not be seen in public. Changes in the behaviour of many motorists are also required. Speeding is an anti-social activity although many people do not see it in this way. A reduction in speed limits would not only make many areas more conducive to walking and prevent some serious injuries and disabilities but also make it safer for vulnerable pedestrians, such as disabled people.

Too many disabled people would appear to be living mainly housebound lives. The British Crime Survey for 2004/05 suggests that one-quarter of disabled people never go out, while in the non-disabled population the figure is 1.5 per cent (Jolly et al. 2006: 59). There is much to welcome in the spread of broadband Internet access and the possibilities of 'virtual mobility' which has allowed many disabled people to work from home and to participate in society, but they should also feel able to travel in their local area. We are still some way from inclusive environments.

As has been noted at various points in this book, not to have access to a car in a car-dependent society can be regarded as a disability. The organization of transport itself also produces disability resulting from the serious injuries from road crashes. Public transport has become more disabled person friendly in recent years but there are still many people with disabilities who cannot use it. As the older population increases in this century there will be more disabled people and it is to that phase of life that we now turn.

Older people

As people age their reactions slow and their sensory abilities, hearing and sight decline. In a car system characterized by speed, high traffic volumes and need to react quickly this can present problems. This is problematic for drivers but also for older people when they are pedestrians and cyclists, putting many of them at some risk, particularly in heavily trafficked areas. In this chapter older people will refer to everyone aged over 50. In 2003 there were 20 million people in the UK over 50 years of age; this figure represents one-third of the population and projections are that it will increase to 41 per cent by 2031 (Soule et al. 2005: 1). The fact that we live in an ageing society has many implications for the transport system. Old age brings with it for many people the onset of disabilities and in the UK fully two-thirds of disabled people are over pensionable age. This chapter examines the linkage between ageing and the way we travel, including the local environment which is so important for older people and shows how the transport choices open to them affect their quality of life.

For older people the car is the most widely used form of transport. Among men, after the age of 17 car driving is the most used mode, reaching its peak in the 50–59 age group where 68 per cent of trips made by men involve the car. This declines slightly to 65 per cent in the 60–69 age group but is still at 57 per cent in the 70+ age range. For women between the ages of 50 and 59, 48 per cent of trip are made by car, while after the age of 60 this figure declines to 34 per cent and over the age of 70 only 16 per cent of trips are made by car (Office for National Statistics 2005). These variations between men and women reflect the differential in licence holding. Women are rapidly catching up with men: in 1975/76 only 29 per cent of women held a driving licence, while in 2006 this had increased to 63 per cent. They still lagged behind men, however, of whom 81 per cent aged over 17 held a driving licence in 2006 (Department for Transport 2008b). Among older people aged over 70 the disparity is most marked: 70 per cent of men hold a driving licence whereas only 27 per cent of women do (Soule et al. 2005: 86). There are currently over 2 million people driving over the age of 70 in Great Britain. This figure will increase in the future with higher rates of licence holders in younger age groups.

With so many older people building their lives around the use of the car in retirement, the vehicle is seen as essential for transporting the heavy food shopping, for visiting friends, for many other kinds of errands, for going on journeys to see family. Many older people who have difficulties with physical mobility are reluctant to stop using their car, as it is their lifeline to the wider world. There can be no doubt that for some elderly motorists driving is something which they would like to do until the day they die; an OECD study concluded that older people with health problems are more likely to give up walking or using public transport than they are driving (OECD 2001). Indeed, there is some evidence that driving cessation can lead to depression (Knight et al. 2007: 78).

Given the centrality of the car in most people's lives the decision to stop driving is not taken lightly. Increasing age can mean that vision deteriorates and this is the most common reason why people decide to stop driving. This is often preceded by a gradual diminution in the number of journeys undertaken. There tends to be a gradual reduction in driving before the decision to hand in one's licence. For example, some people might decide that they will dispense with night-time driving. Older drivers understandably fear a loss of independence, choice and freedom (Rabbitt et al. 2002). This would include being able to spend days out with their families or friends, ability to work if they so chose, and convenience (Gilhooly et al. 2002). This is, after all, what the car has promised and for many people delivered. Unsurprisingly, the loss of independence is felt most keenly by those who have been most reliant on the car in their lives (Knight et al. 2007: 86). The major reasons for the decision to stop driving are: declining health, the general effects of ageing, the loss of the enjoyment of driving, and financial concerns (Knight et al. 2007: 75). Many older drivers who have been driving for some time gained their driving experience in quite different traffic conditions, vehicles and road systems (Rabbitt et al. 2002).

In the UK, once a driver reaches the age of 70 they are required to renew their licence and to notify the Driver and Vehicle Licensing Agency (DVLA) if they have a medical condition which in their opinion will affect their ability to drive.

The DVLA will then assess whether the driver should be allowed to continue. Licences after age 70 are only renewed for three years. However, there is room here for a driver not to notify the authorities and to carry on driving as no medical examination is required. But should this be the case? If someone starts to drive at age 17 then it takes fifty-three years before they have to declare by law whether they have a medical condition which might impair their driving ability. This is a very long time and allows for many medical conditions to occur. But a distinction needs to be made between a medical examination and a driving test. Some would argue that the latter is more needed for older drivers as they might have forgotten some of the Highway Code.

Yet there is a strong argument that a compulsory driving test at age 70 for all drivers is a form of age discrimination. Why should it be for people at a certain age and not, rather, a test of driving ability?

A number of drivers who commit motoring offences might be better candidates for a second driving test than all drivers aged 70. To an extent the argument revolves around safety. There is some evidence that older drivers begin to reduce their driving some time before they finally decide to hand in their licence (Help the Aged 2008).

Many suburbs are built on the assumption that households will have a car, and this makes the decision to stop driving that much more difficult. Elderly people deprived of a car can find themselves virtually housebound if there is not a decent bus service; they may have to rely on expensive taxis in order to carry out essential activities such as shopping or visiting the doctor. Although there are now services which did not exist twenty years ago such as internet grocery shopping with delivery, this does not provide social contact.

Gender is an important consideration when considering transport and older people. In earlier generations, if there was one car in the household then this tended to be monopolized by the man: he took it to work during the day and left his wife to use public transport. This pattern continues when the man retires. If the wife does not drive then the death of her driver husband can mean that she is deprived of transport. Younger generations of women who have much higher levels of car ownership view the car as vital for their independence so that this gender imbalance will not necessarily continue in old age although financial pressures may mean that many couples may decide to forgo two cars in favour of one.

Some men regard driving as central to their masculine identity so that to lose the ability to drive can seem like emasculation. 'Now I consider myself a person. If I stop driving then it means I am not a person any more' (Knight et al. 2007: 80). In Judith Davey's study of older people in New Zealand who had given up driving it was the over 80s on whom the decision had the most impact and particularly for males. She quotes one man as saying that the loss of his ability to drive 'was like cutting off an arm or a leg' (Davey 2007: 54). Davey believes that the greater impact on men derives from the fact that women have more home-based interests and better social networks.

The existence of alternative forms of transport becomes crucial when older people give up their car. It is at this point that many of them make the decision to move to accommodation which is well served by public transport or is within walking distance of shops and other important facilities. Their 'mobility history' becomes important at this point in that their knowledge and experience of buses and trains will have some influence on how well they adjust.

Public transport

The decline of public transport has made the mode less attractive as a travel option for all groups in society, including older people. It might be that some older people are more critical about the state of public transport because they remember an era where buses were much more plentiful and were used by large numbers of people.

Concessionary fares for pensioners and disabled people have been offered by local government for many years but one of the problems was that they varied from one local authority to the next, with the most generous subsidizing free travel for their pensioners. The Transport Act 2000 introduced a subsidy from government to local authorities enabling them to offer half-price off-peak bus travel. (This subsidy is then paid by the local authority to the bus companies.) Since April 2008 everyone aged 60 and over, together with all registered disabled people, has been able to travel free on buses in England after 9.30 am. Similar schemes had been introduced some years before in Scotland and Wales. This is an example of positive age discrimination which is undoubtedly popular but it does raise questions. The obvious one is that many people aged over 60 do not need to travel free on grounds of income while there is the related question as to whether the £1 billion which the bus pass scheme costs in subsidy each year is the best use of a limited transport budget.

If the scheme does make bus travel more attractive, leading to some people choosing to leave the car at home, then there is an obvious environmental benefit. Yet this national off-peak concessionary fare scheme does not help many frail elderly people. Not all older people are able to use buses: those with disabilities may not be able to board the bus or walk to the bus stop or stand waiting for a bus. For those older people who live in rural areas, there are no or very few buses to use. Around fifty local authorities have a travel token scheme which enables pensioners to choose between a free bus pass or a certain amount of tokens which can be used for taxis. At present this is not supported by the government and has to be financed from local authority revenues. The London boroughs finance a Taxicard scheme which provides a certain number – this depends on the borough in which a person lives – of heavily subsidized taxi journeys each year. The Taxicard is only for those with long-term mobility problems who find it difficult to use public transport. To qualify, a person must either be receiving the higher rate of mobility allowance, the higher rate of attendance allowance, be registered blind or receive the mobility supplement with their war pension. These schemes are important because they do reach those who have the most severe mobility problems and need to use a taxi. There is a case to be made that government support for pensioner mobility should be focused on those with the most severe mobility difficulties rather than being distributed to all pensioners, many of whom will drive their own car and are on higher incomes. It is interesting that when Help the Aged surveyed pensioners in Portsmouth who had applied for travel concessions (before the national scheme was introduced), a majority had opted for travel tokens rather than bus passes (Help the Aged 2007).

The problems which older people face in using buses include the height of step up on to the bus, bus stops where there is no seating or shelter from the elements, timetables that are difficult to read and bus drivers who accelerate away from the stop before passengers are seated. Just over half the bus fleet in the UK is now fully accessible, with low floor entry, room for wheelchairs and highly visible grab rails. Although car manufacturers are very receptive to the needs of older drivers there have been criticisms of public transport operators not listening to older people's views, with numerous instances of older people complaining about the negative attitudes of bus drivers towards them. Among barriers to the use of buses and trains is the fear of crime, particularly at night, which has meant that many older people do not travel on public transport in the evenings. In this category one would have to include the yobbish anti-social behaviour of some bus passengers. It has been the case in some parts of the country that bus companies have withdrawn services to certain areas because of this. Scheduled bus services which carry a high number of school children are also avoided by many older people because of the children's bad behaviour and foul language (see Box 9.1). A number of older people's organizations have argued that some of this could be prevented if buses had conductors again. Although conductors are to be reintroduced on some routes in London it is unlikely that bus companies in other parts of the country will follow suit.

Community transport

Community transport is the name given to the range of minibus services which operate throughout the country funded by voluntary organizations. In some areas the organizations supply demand-responsive services which will take people from their door to wherever they wish to travel. In rural areas community transport is sometimes the only bus service available and will be subsidized by the local authority. Community transport drivers are trained to work with disabled people and older people with mobility difficulties, helping passengers board the vehicle, waiting until all are seated before starting the vehicle, carrying shopping from the bus to the door. Nonetheless there is resistance among some older people to using community transport because they feel it stigmatizes them (Knight et al. 2007: 36).

Box 9.1 'Bus is attacked by 30 yobs'

A gang of 30 yobs swarmed round a bus and started attacking the vehicle as terrified passengers looked on in horror.

The youths targeted the number 12 Brighton and Hove bus, which was parked at Newhaven train station.

The quick-thinking bus driver closed the doors to stop any of the yobs clambering on board. No one was injured during the incident.

The driver then managed to get away from the yobs.

The bus was damaged in the attack.

Officers based at Newhaven police station were called to the incident but arrived soon after the bus had left.

Police are now trawling through CCTV footage from the area and from the bus to try and establish who was responsible for the attack, which happened at about 10.10 pm on Saturday.

Managing director of the Brighton and Hove Bus and Coach Company, Roger French, said: 'I'm very concerned to hear about this.

'On this occasion we are co-operating with the police to try and get the CCTV images to them to try and identify the culprits.

'It's absolutely terrible.

Such behaviour is despicable and I hope the culprits are caught and are severely dealt with.'

Source: Richard Gurner, *The Argus* (Brighton), 11 November 2008

Walking

Walking is an important form of exercise as well as transport. It is a way to maintain good health and, as recent Department of Health advice is that adults should engage in physical activity of at least half an hour a day, walking is a good way to achieve this target. Apart from its impact on fitness levels, regular walking has also been shown in some studies to reduce the risk of dementia (Tanne 2004). Unfortunately, some older people decide that the state of their local pavements means that they will not venture forth to use them. A much greater amount of public money is expended on roads than on pavements yet pavements and walkways are vital for short journeys where most journeys are made on foot. Pavements have been neglected by local authorities over the years to the extent that the Audit Commission reports that 24 per cent of local authorities have pavements which are in an unsatisfactory state of repair (Audit Commission 2007). Dunbar et al. (2004: 21) cite government figures from the early 1990s which suggested that as many as ten times as many people attend hospital accident and emergency departments because of falls on the footpath as were injured in vehicle accidents.

Why this matters is that older people can easily fall on cracked and broken pavements. Falls are a major cause of injury for older people – a major cause of disability in people aged over 65 and a major cause of mortality in those who are over the age of 75 (Millward et al. 2003: 31).

Understandably, those in the oldest age group, people over the age of 85, are at the most risk of falling, while the average age to incur a hip fracture is 80. As Easterbrook et al. (2002: 3) comment: 'Fear of falling, and the fear of undertaking tasks or activities that might lead to a fall can lead older people to become disempowered, more isolated and with a reduced quality of life.' Visual impairment is a strong predictor of likelihood to fall (Millward et al. 2003: 32). Visually impaired older people also have difficulty keeping on their feet when confronted with A-boards, cars parked on the pavement, and other obstructions. Of course, not all falls occur on the streets; more than half are in the home (Cryer 2001: 3).

Our growing sedentary lifestyle is exacerbating the conditions which will lead to more falls in the future. Among the over 50 age group, the recommended 30 minutes a day of moderate physical activity is achieved by only one in four men and only one in six women (Cryer 2001: 4). Three million people in the UK have osteoporosis, the bone condition characterized by low bone density and a deterioration of bone tissue, which makes them more likely to suffer a fracture if they fall. Most of these people will be over 50. Standard Six of the National Service Framework for Older People is devoted to falls and their prevention. It states that the aim is to 'reduce the number of falls which result in serious injury and ensure effective treatment and rehabilitation for those who have fallen' (Department of Health 2001: 76). Although the Framework document advises that the local health service should work with local councils on falls prevention this is a reference to social care and social work rather than the transport departments of local authorities who are responsible for the condition of the pavements.

Older pedestrians are at their most vulnerable where they cross the street. Over 90 per cent of pedestrian casualties occur while crossing the street (Cryer 2001: 6). It is at this point that the slower reactions of older people, accompanied by poor eyesight and possibly hearing loss can prove dangerous, even life threatening. The increase in speeds on both urban and rural roads over the past fifty years puts older pedestrians at risk of injury. The consequence is that half of pedestrian deaths are among older people. Even at pelican crossings the time allowed to cross the road is insufficient for some older people.

Unfortunately, the likelihood is that deaths and serious injuries among older drivers will increase in number given the projected increase in the number of older people driving and the fragility of their bodies compared with younger drivers.

Quality of life

Invariably, surveys of older people's attitudes and aspirations find that one of their expectations of the good life is that they will be able to 'get out and about'. The determination of so many older people to keep driving is proof of this. But as we have noted, the ability of non-drivers to travel has decreased with the reduction in bus service levels. All older people – whether they are drivers or not – are at risk from unsafe environments, and the evidence on falls suggests that these are widespread. Much has been written about the need to reinvigorate and revive public spaces in towns and cities. In part this is to do with what the Commission for the Built Environment terms 'civilizing streets', that is to say, seeing them as places rather than merely as thoroughfares for traffic and thus becoming more inclusive public spaces. Holland et al. found, however, that older people felt themselves excluded from public spaces, especially at night. Poor transport after 6 pm was one of the key reasons for this (Holland et al. 2007: 40).

Unfortunately, visits to hospitals and GPs become more important as people reach the latter part of their lives, and here too there is a real problem for older non-drivers who find it difficult to access these facilities. Physical activity is an important way to keep healthy for older people, as for all ages, yet too often the local environment does not support this. Fewer than 2 per cent of trips made by older people over the age of 60 are made by bicycle, yet in Holland, with its safe cycleways, the figure is 20 per cent (Metz 2003: 383).

The concessionary fare schemes which now give free bus travel to everyone aged over 60 in the UK will clearly promote greater mobility among the older population. Yet those who are too disabled to use buses will not benefit.

Accessible environments are those where children, disabled people and those with mobility problems feel that they can use them without fear. This has to be an objective, and transport can play an important role in achieving it. If older people can remain mobile then they are more likely to live for a longer period in their own homes, without the need to go into residential care. Walking is important for older people's health, their use of local facilities and to access public transport.

Well connected: sustainable transport and social policy

In a (hyper)mobile world, transport plays a critical role in linking people, information, goods and resources, yet the evidence is clear that our contemporary forms of personal transport have played a major part in excluding certain groups from participation in society. Poor or non-existent transport has exacerbated existing inequalities whether these be those of age, disability, gender or race. This book has taken a life course approach to illuminate the relationship between transport, mobility and everyday life but the same findings would have resulted from a focus on health, housing, social care or employment. The car system has created health and social problems which disproportionately affect those who do not benefit from access to a car: for example, traffic deaths and serious accidents and traffic-related air and noise pollution. Social cohesion is damaged by 'community severance' resulting from heavily trafficked roads in urban areas while social isolation is exacerbated by poor or non-existent public transport in rural and semi-rural areas. For many years these and other kinds of transport disadvantage were ignored by government although this is no longer the case. The emphasis on social exclusion was official recognition of the way in which state services had sometimes failed to connect with their users. Following the influential Social Exclusion Unit report on transport (2003), local authorities have been tasked with the requirement to look at the accessibility of services. While this was a welcome development this book has shown that the problems are greater and wider than can be encompassed by local authority activity. The environmental consequences of a car-based society and economy are becoming clearer each year as the evidence on global warming and climate change mounts. The system of automobility is an integral part of capitalist society stretching from the state aid given to ailing motor corporations to the personal identification of motorists with their vehicles. The questions posed by critics of automobility are on the mainstream political agenda although they are central to a green critique of contemporary society (see Paterson 2007). This chapter has two aims: to assess the contribution that sustainable transport can make to the problems which climate change will produce and to examine the role of transport in a social policy informed by questions of social justice.

Sustainable transport

The Department for Transport's five goals (Box 10.1) show that there is now official recognition of the contribution that transport can make to equality of opportunity, tackling climate change, quality of life and the health of the population (Department for Transport 2008a). Reading this list one could conclude that sustainable transport is now a reality but this would be to ignore the government's transport policy record over the past decade. A recent analysis came to the conclusion that Labour has just not been interested enough in sustainable transport to take the political risks necessary to push through changes in the organization of transport and the way in which we travel (Docherty and Shaw 2008: 21). Despite the fact that the 1998 White Paper *A New Deal for Transport* was written using the vocabulary of sustainability, within a few years there was a renewed commitment to road building, and road pricing measures were relegated to a future policy agenda. Road pricing, a proven means of encouraging drivers to consider alternative transport choices, remains a policy for the future, especially so given the decisive rejection in December 2008 by the citizens of Greater Manchester of the proposed congestion charge for that city. Government caution had already been strengthened by the vote against a congestion

---

Box 10.1 Department for Transport's five goals

- To support national economic competitiveness and growth by delivering reliable and efficient transport networks.
- To reduce transport's emissions of carbon dioxide and other greenhouse gases, with the desired outcome of tackling climate change.
- To contribute to better safety, security and health and longer life expectancy by reducing the risk of death, injury or illness arising from transport and by promoting travel modes that are beneficial to health.
- To promote greater equality of opportunity for all citizens; with the desired outcome of achieving a fairer society.
- To improve quality of life for transport users and non-transport users, and to promote a healthy natural environment.

Source: Department for Transport 2008a: 12

charge by the citizens of Edinburgh and the 1.7 million people who supported the anti-road pricing petition on the No. 10 website. Underlying the government's reluctance to give a clear lead to the electorate is its fear of alienating 'middle England', the voters who switched their allegiance from the Conservatives in 1997 and have stayed with Labour in the two subsequent elections. The fear of 'middle England' was displayed early in the life of the Blair government when some of the proposals in *A New Deal for Transport* were deleted and has been seen subsequently with the renewed commitment to road building. The government has been anxious to show that it was not 'anti-motorist' which the popular press is ever ready to claim.

Sustainable transport has been defined as transport which meets the needs of the present without compromising the ability of future generations to meet their own transport needs. This means that, strictly speaking, walking and cycling are the only sustainable modes. Public transport is *more* sustainable than the car as it has the capacity to carry a lot more people and thus reduce car use but walking and cycling are the *most* sustainable modes (Tolley 2003). Electric cars and cars powered by hydrogen cells also count as more sustainable transport although they have minimal impact at present (Metz 2008: ch. 8). In its most frequent use it means no more than greater use of the modes of cycling, walking and public transport. Generally, government pronouncements on transport subscribe to the idea of 'sustainable transport'. If one was being cynical this could be characterized as: everyone to walk a little bit more, get on their bicycle for some journeys and to use public transport whenever they can. In other words, marginal change in a car-dominated transport system. This will not be enough if attention is to be properly paid to the needs of future generations, mainly the problems caused by an oil-based and car-dependent transport system. Indeed, there are strong arguments that major changes in how we organize transport should occur within the short term if we are to avoid dangerous rises in temperatures later in the century. The implications for policy are wide ranging for they involve a range of policy issues which include changing land-use planning to ensure that developments in housing or retailing or employment are aligned with good public transport access and taxation policies to encourage less use of the car, with a shift from vehicle excise duty to road pricing and congestion charging.

Climate change and transport policy

The UK government has committed itself to a target of reducing carbon emissions by 80 per cent – on a 1990 baseline – by 2050, and the Climate Change Act 2008 established a mechanism to monitor this. This target means that the transport sector will have to significantly reduce its reliance on fossil fuels. Road transport produces a large part of the UK's carbon emissions accounting for 93 per cent of domestic transport emissions, while 99 per cent of transport is powered by the non-renewable resource of oil (Commission for Integrated Transport 2007: 21). Government is seeking to achieve its climate change targets with some substitution using biofuels, improving the technology of cars so that they do not use so much fuel and supporting efforts to introduce non-carbon-producing fuels together with measures which will encourage people to use alternatives to the car.

Transport is one of the major sources of carbon contributing to global warming. Despite the success of other sectors of the economy in reducing their output of carbon on 1990 figures in line with the Kyoto agreement, in the period 1990–2006 transport actually saw its carbon emissions increase by 12 per cent. Private vehicle use is largely responsible for this increase, with emissions from private vehicles increasing by 30 per cent over this period (Department for Transport 2009b). Although at present aviation contributes a modest amount of the carbon emissions it is going to be increasingly important as a carbon emitter, as the Aviation White Paper has outlined a scenario of continued growth in air travel over the next twenty years (Department for Transport 2003a). Bows and Anderson (2007) concluded that this was a case of 'policy clash' as projected aviation growth could not be reconciled with carbon reduction targets by 2050.

There are various measures which can be taken by government to achieve carbon reduction in the transport sphere. One is to make sure that new cars emit less carbon, and there are EU targets on this. Motorists can, by their driving techniques, reduce the amount of carbon their vehicle emits by using 'eco-driving': keeping within the speed limits, for example. Equally important is for motorists to reduce their use of the car, and this is where the Smarter choices idea becomes important (Commission for Integrated Transport 2007). (See Box 10.2.)

Box 10.2 Smarter choices/soft measures

- Workplace travel plans
- School travel plans
- Personalized travel planning
- Public transport information and marketing
- Travel awareness campaigns
- Car clubs
- Car sharing
- Teleworking
- Teleconferencing
- Home shopping

Source: Cairns et al. 2004

Smarter choices/soft measures are the next step up from educational and marketing campaigns and they involve the use of incentives to get people to change their way of travelling, so the measures can be said to be more targeted than public travel awareness campaigns in that instead of exhortation they focus on individuals and their journeys. Individual travel planning involves a one-to-one discussion which looks at all the main journeys undertaken by a person each week to see whether some of these could be made by non-car transport. Other smart/soft measures include: car sharing, car clubs, teleworking, teleconferencing and school transport plans. The government's spin doctors insisted that soft measures be rebranded as 'smarter choices' and has encouraged local transport departments to implement them. Yet by 2007 only 27 per cent of local authorities had implemented a 'smarter choices' package of measures (Commission for Integrated Transport 2007).

Sloman has a 40:40:20 rule by which she means that 40 per cent of car trips could have been made on foot, by bicycle or public transport without any need for new provision, 40 per cent can only be driven because distances are too great to walk or too difficult to cycle or there is no bus, while 20 per cent of trips need to be made by car because of the nature of the journey, say carrying a sick person or heavy goods (Sloman 2006: 47). In their study *Smarter Choices*, Cairns et al. concluded that a 'high intensity' use of these measures would produce a nationwide reduction in traffic of about 11 per cent, whereas in peak periods in urban areas the reduction would be of the order of 21 per cent (Cairns et al. 2004: 362). Even so, there is some dispute as to how much carbon would be saved (Banks et al. 2007: 26).

Smarter choices can be successful when they reduce the amount of traffic on the roads yet their effect would be negated if the freed road space was used by other drivers taking the place of those who had decided to walk, cycle or use the bus. There are various ways to try to prevent this happening: road space can be reallocated so that, for example, a cycleway is built or pavements are widened.

Aside from traffic engineering schemes which could significantly reduce the number of journeys made on the roads there are fiscal measures such as taxes on fuel and vehicles. Congestion charging has worked in London having led to a reduction of over 21 per cent in traffic entering the central area (Transport for London n.d.), but government has adopted a 'softly softly' approach to congestion charging and road pricing for fear of alienating motorists and their votes. Despite its recognition of the enormous threat posed to the British way of life by climate change, the government still seems reluctant to give a lead on measures to reduce carbon emissions. Carbon reduction is seen as one of its priorities but not the main priority.

Road pricing is on the agenda – the long-term agenda admittedly – of the government but measures to deal with carbon emissions might well start to impinge upon government transport policy with far greater bite. Road pricing is one way of reducing carbon emissions but it is mainly regarded by government as a way of reducing congestion.

Road pricing is socially regressive if it is a flat rate tax on the use of certain roads as motorists on low incomes would find it a greater burden than others. Already motoring costs are higher for them: driving accounts for 24 per cent of the weekly expenditure of those households in the lowest income quintile who have a car as compared with only 15 per cent for all motorists in the UK (Social Exclusion Unit 2003). The inequity can be reduced, but not abolished, by such means as charging more for larger vehicles and more polluting vehicles. The revenues from road pricing could be spent on public transport services, principally buses, hence benefiting those on low incomes more than some other groups in the population. Grayling et al. commissioned research which outlined two scenarios. The first scenario was revenue neutral, that is to say, road pricing did not raise any more in taxation than before it was introduced as other taxes on motoring were reduced or abolished. The second scenario was a congestion charge which raised revenue. The revenue-neutral scenario resulted in an overall increase in traffic of around 7 per cent and an increase in carbon emissions of 5 per cent. London would be the only region to see an overall decrease in traffic. The second scenario, the revenue-raising one, however, would cut traffic by 7 per cent and carbon emissions by 8 per cent. All regions would see a decrease in traffic (Grayling et al. 2004). The authors of the study proposed that the vehicle excise duty – the car tax – be abolished on the grounds that it was flat rate and unrelated to the number of times a vehicle was used. Road pricing might also reduce the number of journeys being made, which would reduce the impact on those low-income communities which live adjacent to busy roads. In rural areas the vehicle excise duty is an unfair tax for households on low incomes where there is less pollution and congestion (Foley and Fergusson 2003).

Changes of this kind are overdue. Motoring taxation has long been in need of reform as motorists are not being taxed on the costs of their pollution and congestion. Pollution consists of not only the carbon emissions but also the fumes which exacerbate and contribute to asthma, stunted lung growth in children and premature death. Disturbing evidence was provided in EU reports early in 2009 that more than 20 cities and conurbations were found to have dangerous levels of particulate matter. 'Air pollution near many roads in British cities averages well over twice the UN's World Health Organization maximum recommended level' (Vidal 2009; also see Swinford 2009).

Speed limits can also be used to reduce carbon emissions. There is a good case to reduce the motorway speed limit to 60 mph for this would reduce car emissions overall by 18 per cent. The proper enforcement of the present 70 mph speed limit would lead to carbon reductions of around 0.45 MtC a year (House of Commons Environmental Audit Committee 2006).

Currently, 56 per cent of drivers exceed the motorway speed limit, with 10 per cent travelling at speeds above 80 mph (Anable and Bristow 2007: 109). The Commission for Integrated Transport advocates what it calls 'eco-driving' as a way to reduce carbon emissions (see Box 10.3).

Box 10.3 What is eco-driving?

Aspects of eco-driving include:

- Accelerating gently, keeping speed constant and changing gear at the optimal time.
- Adhering to speed limits.
- Limiting the use of air conditioning.
- Reducing drag by driving with the windows closed and empty roof racks removed.
- Avoiding idling the engine.
- Not warming the engine up before starting off.
- Ensuring the tyres are filled to the optimum pressure.
- Shedding excess weight from the car.
- Keeping a safe distance from the car in front.

Source: Commission for Integrated Transport 2007: 61

Given the extent of carbon emissions from transport, considerable effort is going into producing low-carbon cars. The trend to make cars much more comfortable with air conditioning, sound systems, electric windows adds to the weight of vehicles, and this again increases the carbon emissions. The hybrid car which uses both electric motor and a petrol engine is an early example of the low-carbon car as it has significantly reduced the amount of petrol used. Various electric cars are now coming on to the market.

Personal carbon allowances have the merit of involving the entire population, just as rationing did during the Second World War, and thus underlining the seriousness of global warming. The personal carbon allowance is a way to reduce carbon emissions and to protect those on low incomes. Each adult would receive a free carbon allowance, with children receiving a smaller allowance – there is some discussion as to whether children should be within the scheme at all – and each person would be allocated a certain number of carbon units which would have to be surrendered whenever they made an energy purchase, that is to say, filled up with petrol, paid their gas bill or travelled on the bus. A market in these allowances would be created, with those leading a carbon-intensive lifestyle able to purchase units off those who had not, in the space of a year, used all their credits. The total amount of the carbon allowances would be reduced each year in line with the government's commitment to reduce carbon emissions.

The advantage of this carbon allowance scheme over carbon taxes is that it enables those who lead low-carbon lifestyles – often those on low incomes – to gain financially from selling their allowances on the market. What it would also do would be to get across to the general public the importance of saving carbon and not using unnecessary amounts of carbon (Hillman and Fawcett 2004). Many of the decisions which result in the release of carbon are made every day by ordinary individuals. Where we choose to take a holiday, how we travel to work, how warm our houses are, how many lights we leave on in our houses – all these mundane examples have consequences for the UK's output of carbon emissions. Governments have been aware for some time that the public needs not only information and education about global warming but incentives to change behaviour towards living a less carbon-intensive lifestyle. It is only a small minority of the population who will voluntarily make major changes in their way of life in response to the growing problems produced by climate change. These are the people who will give up their car, or pledge not to fly, in order to reduce their carbon footprint.

Although small, it is true that their numbers have been growing in recent years as is evident from the spread of the transition towns movement. This movement aims to equip people with the skills they will need to cope in a world where oil is an extremely scarce resource. This has led to food cultivation projects, sewing and knitting classes, renewable energy schemes and other initiatives (Hopkins 2008). Interesting as these projects are they will only ever attract a minority of the population whereas the UK needs to see the majority of the population change their behaviour in order to reduce carbon emissions. This is a tall order as it might be said that consumer society is based around wants being perceived as needs and the market can supply these. Usually the resource consequences of purchasing decisions are not reflected in the price paid for goods. For some time environmentalists have urged government to move taxation policy towards taxing environmental 'bads' but this has not happened to any great extent. Indeed, as we have noted, the one significant environmental tax in transport, the fuel price escalator, had to be abandoned given the hostility of the public with the fuel protests in 2000.

Car ownership has entered deeply into the national psyche. Automobility 'is central to the individualist, consumerist affective culture of contemporary capitalism' (Urry 2007: 265). For more than half a century it has been an uncontested premise that individuals should be free to drive whenever and wherever they choose. Lorenzoni et al. (2007: 453) highlight the high status given to cars plus the impact of habitual behaviour: 'Socially-acceptable ways of behaving – for example, driving to work, frequent long-haul holidays and weekend breaks, leaving appliances on and the weekly supermarket shop – in turn become ingrained as unconscious habitual behaviours, making them unquestioned and thus more intractable.' To begin to change the mindset which sees driving – and flying – as a personal freedom is a major challenge. Especially when, as we have seen, governments encouraged the demand for personal car ownership and 'predict and provide' policies of successive governments supplied the necessary road space. The fact that Britain is a small island which cannot build many more roads to accommodate even more cars and the reality of carbon emissions exacerbating global warming mean that governments have to persuade the public to use their cars less and to change their driving behaviour. (For an alternative view which recommends more road building together with a national system of road pricing, see Banks et al. 2007.)

Car advertising is just the most visible part of a very successful lobby for cars which has a seemingly unchallengeable position in British national life. In the 1960s and 1970s, as British motor manufacturers succumbed to foreign car competition, the car industry was seen as vital to the national interest and the inefficiencies and poor design seen as an aspect of British economic decline. The creation of British Leyland was a 1970s 'old Labour' response by creating a publicly owned car firm. So too in the current recession have motor manufacturers turned to the state for support. It is not difficult to sketch the power which automobility has in the UK. In the criminal justice system crimes committed by motorists have been treated more leniently than if the culprit had not been behind the wheel of a car (Corbett 2003). Large numbers of motorists openly admit that they break speed limits. The appeal of the car derives from the fact it has provided a personalized, secure and comfortable means of travelling although, as we have noted in this book, its impact on the human body has been unwelcome, not just the road casualties and fatalities but also the decline in physical activity which results from a car-dependent lifestyle.

To reach a number of policy goals discussed in this book government has to persuade the public that there has to be a significant reduction in car use, which will require a substantial change in behaviour. The analogy has been made with smoking – it has been known since the 1950s that smoking causes lung cancer but it was to take fifty years before smoking came to be considered anti-social enough to be banned in public places (Docherty and Shaw 2008: 21). But it seems unlikely that we have half a century to reduce carbon emissions significantly – there are strong arguments that radical reductions will need to occur over the next decade in transport if the government is to meet its carbon emissions targets.

Reviewing public attitudes to transport and climate change Anable et al. reported that although there was a high level of public concern about climate change it was not thought to be an immediate problem which would impinge upon the respondents' own lives; rather it was more of a problem for future generations. Indeed, transport was the least acceptable area for action on climate change (Anable et al. 2006a). Lorenzoni et al. point out that while the great majority of the UK public understand the reasons for climate change this understanding has little effect on their behaviour, with energy demand rising in both the domestic and transport sectors of the economy. In contrast to the view of the UK government the UK public regard many other environmental issues as more important than climate change. In 2004 the Energy Saving Trust found that 85 per cent of UK residents believed the effects of climate change would not be seen for decades (Lorenzoni et al. 2007: 447). Stradling et al. (2008: 148–9) found that 23 per cent of drivers agreed with the statement 'People should be allowed to use their cars as much as they like, even if it causes damage to the environment', while only 21 per cent of respondents – drivers and non-drivers – supported the idea of motorists paying higher taxes for the sake of the environment.

This is despite the fact that governments and local authorities have pursued educational campaigns for some time alerting the public to the environmental and health consequences of the way we travel, schemes such as Travelwise, Walk To School, Car Free Days. All the while the numbers of people cycling and walking have declined and the number of cars on the roads has increased. But is this surprising given the small sums spent on these campaigns when compared with the vast advertising budgets of car manufacturers? However, Stradling et al. did find support for the proposition among drivers that they should cut down on car use for short journeys, that is journeys of under two miles. Forty-five per cent of drivers agreed with this (Stradling et al. 2008: 153).

Government policy on sustainable transport is written from an environmental modernization perspective: cars can be greened, emissions can be reduced sufficiently to avoid catastrophic climate change, all can aspire to be motorists but we must use our cars less. An alternative radical green perspective holds that the system of automobility, with all its attendant sprawl and public health problems, is a major contributor to the economic and social overdevelopment which imperils life on the planet. This perspective looks to a 'post car' future where the environmentally benign modes of cycling and walking are as normal and widely practised as car driving is today.

Walking

Walking has been described as the 'acid test' for the sustainable transport policy of the government (Tolley in Docherty and Shaw 2003: 178). With the need to reduce carbon emissions substantially, walking will need to regain its place as a major transport mode. However, between 1995/97 and 2005 the average number of walk trips per person fell by 16 per cent from 292 to 245 per year (Department for Transport 2007d).

Increasing the amount of walking will necessitate a big improvement in the walking environment and public space making it much more attractive for people to walk. This will entail greater spending on pavements and walkways to ensure that people do not trip or slip. Many streets are not hospitable to walking as on-street car parking removes space which would be used for other purposes. Pavement parking not only removes space but also presents a hazard for many, especially those with mobility problems. There are some roads where crossing is virtually impossible because they are so congested with traffic or where vehicles travel at high speeds. These can be likened to rivers in the physical landscape as they fracture neighbourhoods. Safer roads and safer pavements highlight the need for greater enforcement by the police of the existing traffic regulations.

More people walking will have benefits for community life. In her classic book *The Death and Life of Great American Cities* the American writer Jane Jacobs (1962) argued that regular, informal contact in the streets supported community life, calling it the 'informal surveillance' of the street. Jacobs was writing about New York in the 1950s and she might have been describing a number of British cities at that time where streets were busy with people. With the motorization of cities many of those people who used to walk along the pavements will now be driving along the roads. When people speak of the loss of community this is one of the elements which has disappeared.

There is a growing recognition that streets are not just thoroughfares for the passage of traffic but are also places where people can meet one another, go about their daily business and, in the best of them, just sit and watch the world go by. The publication by government of the planning advice *Manual for Streets* in 2007 was a welcome step forward in this process. It is designed to bring about 'a transformation in the quality of streets' aiming to create streets that

- help to build and strengthen the communities they serve
- meet the needs of all users, by embodying the principles of inclusive design
- form part of a well-connected network
- are attractive and have their own distinctive identity
- are cost-effective to construct and maintain and
- are safe.

(Department for Transport 2007c: 1.1.5)

Many European cities have grappled with the problems caused by cars in the urban environment and some have shown the way in which walking can be restored to a central place in the organization of public space.

Measures to boost walking have to be part of an overall plan to reduce the dangers from motor vehicles. This involves slower speeds, traffic engineering to make the road safer for pedestrians and better enforcement to ensure that cars do not park on pavements.

Although government has advised local authorities that they should give greater priority to walking and cycling in their local transport plans, in the absence of a national walking strategy and national targets local authorities might be forgiven for wondering if, in fact, government is strongly committed to walking.

The priority given to cars in urban planning makes walking journeys more dangerous and less pleasant. There are innumerable possible journeys on foot, particularly in urban areas, which are not undertaken because of the fear of crossing a dangerous road or the unpleasant nature of a walking trip in over-congested streets. Walking has to be linked to land-use planning, however. More walking trips 'repopulate' urban areas. But a revival of walking will have to be linked to different ideas of land use, for in many areas there is literally nowhere to walk to. Suburban areas are notorious for their absence of shops and facilities which can be reached on foot, for people need a destination or a purpose if they are to walk. There are too many people living in suburbs from which their inhabitants can only reach facilities by car.

While one can imagine that more people can be persuaded via incentives to use public transport it is less straightforward to see how this can apply to suburban parts of the country where densities are low. If household density is less than 50 houses per hectare then there are insufficient people for small shops to open or for a bus service to run. Unfortunately the trend in house building has been for houses with gardens in low-density areas.

Increasing walking is important not only on environmental grounds to reduce carbon emissions but also, as we have seen, for reasons of public health as it is an excellent form of physical exercise. One of the major causes of the decline in physical activity stems from the way in which walking has been designed out of everyday life, with fewer people using public transport which invariably involves a walking journey. The revival of walking as a major transport mode requires the taming of the car, which involves a series of measures such as reduced traffic speeds, continuous walkways not bisected by roads, and lower speeds. These pedestrian priority measures need to be throughout residential areas as well as in city and town centres.

Cycling

The National Cycling Strategy was quite clear about the benefits of cycling: 'It offers a widely accessible, convenient and environmentally-friendly means of making local journeys, especially in urban and suburban areas. And it is a healthy, enjoyable, economic and efficient means of travelling' (Department of Transport 1996: 2). The National Cycling Strategy of 1996 set out some ambitious targets: by the end of 2002 it envisaged a doubling of the number of trips by bicycle on 1996 figures and by it foresaw a quadrupling of the number of trips by bicycle by the end of 2012. The 2002 target was not achieved and the 2012 target has been scaled back. Indeed, following the publication of the cycling strategy, over the period from 1995/96 to 2005 the average number of trips by bicycle fell by 22 per cent from 18 to 14 trips per person per year (Department for Transport 2007d). This is an indication of the task involved in getting more people on to their bicycles.

Yet London has bucked this trend with the average annual increase in cycle trips of around 17 per cent (Transport for London 2008: 1). The central London congestion charge has obviously been a big boost to cycling in the capital city highlighting the fact that to enable more people to feel that it is safe for them to get on their bicycles a range of related measures needs to be put in place such as slower speeds and more road space for cyclists.

The National Cycling Strategy of 1996 set out the sustainability benefits, which would accrue from more cycling in the UK (Box 10.4).

Box 10.4 Sustainability benefits from cycling

Cycling can contribute to a wide range of sustainability benefits. To achieve them the National Cycling Strategy will seek to:

- Encourage more people to cycle and so reduce pollution, enhance local environments and improve health and social care
- Secure a shift from cars to bicycles, while ensuring that the space released is not filled up by more cars
- Increase accessibility to amenities and services by bicycle
- Make cycling safer

Source: Department of Transport 1996

The number of cycling trips is way below those for walking or driving. Why this should have happened is a reflection of a number of causes but among them is the fear that many people have of cycling on busy roads with high densities of cars. In urban areas cyclists require their own protected space and in other countries, such as the Netherlands, segregated cycleways are the norm. A low-carbon transport system will need to invest heavily in cycling and cycling provision with reallocation of road space to cycling-only lanes, which are secure from invasion by motor vehicles. Seventy-three per cent of journeys are less than five miles and 47 per cent are less than two miles, so the potential for cycling is clearly there. Added to this is the fact that there are more cycles than cars in the UK. Yet the UK lags far behind many of its European neighbours in the cycling statistics. Only 2 per cent of children cycle to school as compared with around 65 per cent in the Netherlands (Department of Transport 1996). As with walking, an increase in cycling will see improvements in the health status of cyclists. Research suggests that a targeted focus on improving cycling as an option can be successful. Wardman et al. report that employers paying a small financial incentive, cycle parking and good shower facilities at work and segregated cycleways would make a real difference in the number of people prepared to cycle to work (Wardman et al. 2007).

Cycling has some of the advantages of car driving but with none of the environmental problems: it enables one to travel from door to door and gives the freedom to decide when and where one wants to travel. Moreover, the bicycle enables those on low incomes to reach a place of employment and has the potential to restore mobility and freedom to many children.

Public transport

For longer distances the real alternative to the private car is public transport, which can of course be reached by walking or cycling, and bicycles can be carried on trains. Public transport is an efficient way of transporting large numbers of people into and out of cities and urban areas. Where it is not so useful is outside of the urban conurbations where development for more than forty years has proceeded on the assumption that most people will have access to a car. This has produced a distribution of housing and employment which is not friendly to public transport. In many areas the population per hectare is insufficient to maintain a bus service. As we have seen, this bears particularly hard on the carless and certain groups in the population. People in households without a car made 20 per cent of their journeys by bus compared with 3 per cent in households with one or more cars (Department for Transport 2006c: 21). Public transport will need to play a much bigger part in a sustainable transport future as car use decreases but it will entail much wider changes than merely increasing the frequency of bus or rail services. It would appear that in relation to bus services it is not so much improvements in bus frequency or routes which would encourage infrequent bus users who are car drivers to use them, rather it would be the difficulties of driving, especially the difficulty in parking. Since the introduction of the congestion charge bus use has increased by 38 per cent during the three-hour morning peak in London (Department for Transport 2006c: 13).

Dedicated bus lanes enable buses to move through congested queuing traffic thus giving them an advantage over the car. Light rail and tram services are another efficient way of moving large numbers of people in and around dense urban areas but their cost, not just the track and engines but the expense of purchasing the land, has reduced their appeal for central and local government.

In the UK the bus has been seen by many people as a second-class form of transport. However, a number of local authorities have shown that this can be tackled and have increased bus usage. A major barrier to doing so is the lack of knowledge in car-dependent households about how to use the buses.

It is not uncommon to come across people who have spent their childhood in car-dependent families never having used a bus.

The bus's decline – in the number of passengers, the number of routes and its status – is the consequence of the ascent of the car over the past half century. But it is a crucial means of transport to link communities and provide access to work. The bus can meet these and other social policy objectives but it is doubtful whether the present system of private provision and public regulation is the best arrangement to achieve these objectives.

Transport is social policy

One could have a sustainable transport system and yet still have major social inequalities. Mobility has become a central motif of our society and those who are 'mobility poor' are not able to enjoy the same opportunities as those who are 'mobility rich'. In preceding chapters we have seen how access to transport is an important theme throughout the lifecycle. To discuss the health service or education or social care services without discussing how people reach these services and, on the other hand, how these services reach their patients, parents and clients, is a strange omission.

As we saw in Chapter 1, transport disadvantage can be fruitfully explored using the framework devised by Jonathan Wolff and Avner De-Shalit in their recent book *Disadvantage* (Wolff and De-Shalit 2007).

Drawing on the work of Sen and Nussbaum they posit that there are functionings – what a person is able to do and to be – and that lack of mobility can reduce our ability to fully engage with others and with society. Mobility has become important for social capital.

Social capital

The role of personal transport has been a feature of the social capital debate which has occupied Whitehall, Washington and the transatlantic policy community at times over the past decade. Social capital is the sum of the networks, informal structures and norms that enable action both individual and collective. Robert Putnam, in his classic text *Bowling Alone*, joins the ranks of those who argue that the dispersal of population into suburbs and the resulting reliance on the car weakens community ties and reinforces privatized lifestyles. For Putnam, the longer the commuting trip the less the social capital enjoyed by the individual. 'Let us act to ensure that by 2010 Americans will spend less time travelling and more time connecting with our neighbours' (Putnam 2000: 407). In the UK, as Halpern notes, commuting weakens communities, reducing the time people can spend with their friends and family (Halpern 2005: 263). For Urry, on the other hand, it is the fact of mobility which enables social capital to grow: mobility acts to provide social interconnectedness and to foster social networks (Urry 2002: 264–5). While there is some truth in this the fact remains that this form of long-distance social networking tends to degrade and weaken the local neighbourhood. Halpern draws out a number of policy conclusions to strengthen social capital which include the promotion of safe playspace for children, Home Zones and making streets into places again (Halpern 2005: 310–11). Transport-related measures of this kind can strengthen social capital and demonstrate that accessible public services should be a citizen's right but they do not cover the entirety of what is needed.

The search for an integrated community and functioning town or city has been a feature of town planning since the nineteenth century. Land use is crucial for transport and in the USA critics of urban sprawl believe it is a major factor in the lifestyle diseases, obesity in particular, which beset the country (Frumkin et al. 2004).

Citizenship

> Car driving has become a central element of social citizenship.
> (Urry 2002: 265)

Although Urry is correct that in car-dependent societies to be without access to a car is going to seriously damage the quality of your life, it cannot be a viable way forward given that car ownership can never be universal, there will always be people who from reasons of disability, choice, age will not be able to drive a car and there will always be people who will not be able – again for a variety of reasons – to gain access to a car. The sobering statistics on the contribution of transport to carbon emissions mean it cannot be a sustainable transport policy option either. This means that public transport becomes important for citizenship. Granted, not everyone can gain access to public transport, some disabled people have problems in reaching bus stops or boarding vehicles so this is an option which will remain closed to them. The dispersed nature of our car-oriented society ensures a significant amount of housing and employment is not served by public transport.

Cities have public spaces and if these public spaces are used by a variety of people, different ages, social class, occupations, then they are an index of social cohesion, a sharing of common life (Wickham 2006b: 5). As we have seen, first the railways, then trams, buses and finally cars enabled people to live at some distance from their place of work which weakened social cohesion. Cars tend to destroy public space as they need more land to become automobilized road space. But, more than this, catering for the needs of the car tends to create single-use spaces, be that a car park or a shopping mall. In contrast, public spaces are multi-use spaces, a park, a square, a market (Wickham 2006b: 6).

There are lessons for sustainable urban development from other European countries regarding public transport. It is important that public transport links are built at the same time as the housing so that residents do not get into a car-commuting habit. Equally – and it is surely one of the roles which a sustainable transport policy should play – those who are carless should know that shopping and other facilities are close to public transport links. If those carless people are on low incomes then this becomes a way to promote social inclusion. Wickham gives the example of Kontula, a working-class suburb of Helsinki, where the metro link was built close to shops and facilities and at the same time as the housing (Wickham 2006b: 111–13).

Citizenship in the context of transport does entail responsibilities as well as rights. This includes the obligation not to behave in an anti-social manner – annoying other passengers with loud music, using offensive language – which is one of the reasons why some people dislike using public transport. As with most responsibilities there is a role for someone to enforce good order and this is why there is a case for the return of bus conductors. It is helpful to think of public transport as an extension of public space so that just as there have to be rules governing behaviour in public spaces so there should be rules for public transport. Public transport, like public spaces, give the possibility of meeting strangers, conversing with strangers or just being with strangers.

The decision by the railway operating companies to stop calling us passengers but to use the term 'customers' was symbolic of the shift from public utility to market, from citizen to consumer. The UK has gone through a major change in the organization of buses and railways which has had mixed results. The deregulation and privatization of buses in the mid-1980s did not arrest the fall in the number of bus passengers (White 2009: 17). The dominant ethos of UK society since the 1980s has been one of individuals acting in their own interests and those of their family with notions of the common good or even society downgraded. The belief has been encouraged that the atomized individual is best able to provide for essential needs such as health, education and transport, and where the individual cannot afford private solutions then the state services should be marketized to give individuals who are thought of as consumers more choice. The state has been downgraded in favour of market solutions such as privatization (Root 2007). The recession following the financial crisis of 2008 has shown the weakness of market-based solutions and it is a moot point whether these will continue to be the best way to provide a transport system which has environmental and social objectives as a priority.

Social justice

We can explore the connections between transport and mobility policy by employing the concept of social justice.

Miller (2005: 5) argues that there are four essential components of social justice:

- Equal citizenship: civil, political and social rights.
- The social minimum: citizens should have access to resources that enable them to meet essential needs and to lead a secure and dignified life.
- Equality of opportunity: a person's life chances should depend upon their own efforts and aptitudes rather than the colour of their skin, their gender or class.
- Fair distribution: resources may be distributed unequally such as income or 'quality of life' factors such as job satisfaction.

If we relate these four components of social justice to the themes of this book starting with citizenship, should we be talking about mobility rights in addition to civil, political and social rights? To the extent that each citizen should be able to use public space for movement for short distances this is a valid case. Pavements and walkways need to be safe and accessible for all, which would include those with mobility handicaps. This would entail an obligation on local government to keep pavements in a good state of repair and an obligation on the police to enforce traffic legislation which would include action against those who park on pavements thereby obstructing them for pedestrians. The damage done to pavements, the broken and cracked paving stones, are usually the result of this anti-social parking. We need to be clear what is being encouraged here. It is for people who have been forced to give up walking around their neighbourhood to be able to do so again because it is a safer environment and moreover because they have a right to do so. The corollary is that for this to occur some motorists would need to behave in more responsible ways by not parking on the pavement, for example, or driving at excessive speeds.

So can we say that transport or mobility citizenship is a social right? There is a latent view of transport as social service which can be seen not just in the recent extension of concessionary fares to all people over the age of 60 but also to the benefits given under the Disability Living Allowance to people with certain disabilities to aid them with their transport costs. There is also a less tangible but nonetheless important feeling that public transport in some senses belongs to us, that we have an entitlement to it. A mobility right is indeed often a means of gaining access to public services.

Central to the vision of those who argued for an extension of the state's role in social welfare provision in the first half of the twentieth century was the idea of a national minimum in education and health. We can make the same claim for transport, that there should be a minimum level of public transport around the country. Again, we have the rudiments of this still surviving today in the subsidies which local authorities pay to local bus companies to provide 'socially necessary' services.

Equality of opportunity is an objective which states and individuals can strive towards which will mean benefits for certain groups but as a concept will never be achieved. Accessibility is key to achieving this in transport (Hine 2008: 50). Take disabled people who cannot drive. They will be able to use other forms of transport which will enable them to reach key destinations such as a workplace but they will not enjoy the flexibility and independence which car ownership provides. The social definition of disability has focused attention on the social and physical barriers which prevent disabled people from playing a fuller part in society. In this example, disabled people are given greater help so that their position, say in relation to getting to work, is improved. At the same time some of these improvements are of benefit to other groups in the society. Room for wheelchairs on buses also means room for pushchairs, for example. It remains true that accessibility has been conceived of by government as access to places and while the various measures put in place to achieve this since the passing of the Disability Discrimination Act 1995 have been useful and beneficial for disabled people, there does remain the problem that more mobile societies operate on the assumption of a high degree of mobility – or connectivity – on the part of citizens (Larsen et al. 2006). Undoubtedly the more prosperous members of society will always have greater access to new technology which can aid their connectivity. Yet the state must have a role in ensuring that new technologies are used to facilitate the network needs of those on low incomes, disabled people and others. Sometimes this is not necessary as diffusion occurs through the market anyway, as with the case of mobile phones. Recent research on the uses of information and communication technologies (ICT) show the potential to connect individuals and communities without the requirement to travel (Kenyon et al. 2002, 2003). This virtual mobility should mean that face-to-face meetings are not required, but as Larsen et al. suggest, ICT tends to encourage more meetings, journeys to see people and places rather than less. Their research leads them to claim that mobile phones and cars are twin technologies which create 'a flexible, modern social life' and in which the access to these technologies produces social inclusion:

> This also means that crucial to the character of modern societies is network capital, comprising, most importantly, access to communication technologies, affordable and well-connected transport and safe meeting-places.
>
> (Larsen et al. 2006: 132)

The last of Miller's components of social justice is fair distribution. Mobility resources reflect the distribution of income and wealth in general but the evidence presented in this book shows that there has been a deterioration in access and mobility for those who are carless. This has consequences for personal and social life which limit what a person can do and be. A fairer distribution of mobility resources would surely involve an expansion of public transport together with more investment in cycling and walking infrastructure. There has been over the past three decades a considerable amount of activity in the USA on transportation issues using the concept of environmental justice where it encompasses discrimination, denial of benefits and adverse effects. This has included the consequences for communities of road building, transport-related air and noise pollution and denial of access to transport (Lucas 2004: 157). There is overlap here with social justice for it is clear that the environmental hazards from transport are unfairly distributed with low-income groups losing out.

Transport and questions of mobility are integral to many issues in social policy. It is also central to everyday life and personal satisfaction.

To be 'well connected' is important for all of us and transport should play a major part in this ensuring that we have the ability to visit friends and family, go to work, pursue our leisure interests and whatever else we want to do. It is central to our well-being.

Further reading

Craig, G., Burchardt, T. and Gordon, D. (eds) (2008). *Social Justice and Public Policy*. Bristol: Policy Press.

Giddens, A. (2009). *The Politics of Climate Change*. Cambridge: Polity Press.

Raje, F. (2004). *Transport, Demand Management and Social Inclusion: The Need for Ethnic Perspectives*. Aldershot: Ashgate Press.

Bibliography

Action for Blind People (2008). *Report on Verbal and Physical Abuse towards Blind and Partially Sighted People across the UK*. London: Action for Blind People.

Adams, J. (1993). Promoting 'safety' through fear. In M. Hillman (ed.), *Children, Transport and the Quality of Life*. London: Policy Studies Institute.

Air Quality Expert Group (2007a). *The Air Quality Strategy for England, Scotland, Wales and Northern Ireland*. London: Defra.

Air Quality Expert Group (2007b). *Air Quality and Climate Change: A UK Perspective. Summary Report*. London: Defra.

Aldred, R. and Woodcock, J. (2008). Transport: challenging disabling environments. *Local Environment*, 13(6): 485–96.

Anable, J. and Bristow, A. L. (2007). *Transport and Climate Change*. London: Commission for Integrated Transport.

Anable, J., Lane, B. and Kelay, T. (2006a). *An Evidence Based Review of Public Attitudes to Climate Change and Transport Behaviour*. London: Department for Transport.

Anable, J., Mitchell, P. and Layberry, R. (2006b). *Getting the Genie Back in the Bottle: Limiting Speed to Reduce Carbon Emissions and Accelerate the Shift to Low Carbon Vehicles*. London: UKERC/Slower Speeds Initiative.

Appleyard, D. (1982). *Livable Streets*. Berkeley: University of California Press.

Audit Commission (2007). *Changing Lanes*. London: Audit Commission.

Bacon, L. (2007). Perceived neglect. *The Guardian*, 8 December.

Bagley, C. (1992). The urban setting of juvenile pedestrian injuries. *Accident Analysis and Prevention*, 24(6): 673–8.

Banks, N., Bayliss, D. and Glaister, S. (2007). *Motoring towards 2050: Roads and Reality*. London: RAC Foundation.

Barclay, P. (1982). *Social Workers: Their Roles and Tasks* (Barclay Report). London: Bedford Square Press.

Barnes, C. and Mercer, G. (2003). *Disability*. Cambridge: Polity Press.

Barrett, E., Heycock, D., Hick, D. and Judge, E. (2003). Issues in access for disabled people: the case of the Leeds transport strategy. *Policy Studies*, 24(4): 227–42.

Barton, H. (2007). Strategic planning. In N. Cavill (ed.), *Building Health: Creating and Enhancing Places for Healthy, Active Lives*. London: National Heart Forum.

Bendixson, T. (1977). *Instead of Cars*. London: Penguin.

Betty, C. and Cahill, M. (1999). British expatriate experience of health and social services on the Costa del Sol. In F. Anthias and G. Laziridis (eds), *Into the Margins: Migration and Exclusion in Southern Europe*. Aldershot: Ashgate Press.

Beunderman, J., Hannon, C. and Bradwell, P. (2007). *Seen and Heard: Reclaiming the Public Realm with Children and Young People*. London: Demos.

Beynon, H. (1973). *Working for Ford*. Harmondsworth: Penguin.

Bishop, S. and Grayling, T. (2003). *The Sky's the Limit: Policies for Sustainable Aviation*. London: Institute for Public Policy Research.

Black, W. R. and Nijkamp, P. (2000). *Social Change and Sustainable Transport*. Bloomington: Indiana University Press.

Böhm, S., Jones, C., Land, C. and Paterson, M. (2006). *Against Automobility*. Oxford: Blackwell.

Bostock, L. (2001). Pathways of disadvantage? *Health and Social Care in the Community*, 9(1): 11–18.

Bows, A. and Anderson, K. (2007). Policy clash: can projected aviation growth be reconciled with the UK government's 60% carbon reduction target? *Transport Policy*, 14(2): 103–10.

Breen, J. (2002). Protecting pedestrians. *British Medical Journal*, 324: 1109–10.

Bristow, D., Pridmore, A., Tight, M. et al. (2004). *How Can We Reduce Carbon Emissions from Transport?* Norwich: Tyndall Centre for Climate Change Research.

British Heart Foundation (2004). *Couch Kids*. London: British Heart Foundation.

British Medical Association (1992). *Cycling towards Health and Safety*. Oxford: Oxford University Press.

Brunton, G., Oliver, S., Oliver, K. and Lorenc, T. (2006). *A Synthesis of Research Addressing Children's, Young People's and Parents' Views of Walking and Cycling for Transport*. London: EPPI-Centre, Social Science Research Unit, Institute of Education, University of London.

Buchanan, C. (1958). *Mixed Blessing: The Motor in Britain*. London: Leonard Hill.

Buchanan, C. (1963). *Traffic in Towns*. London: Penguin Books in association with HMSO.

Burchardt, T., Le Grand, J. and Piachaud, D. (2002). Degrees of exclusion: developing a dynamic, multidimensional measure. In J. Hills, J. Le Grand and D. Piachaud (eds), *Understanding Social Exclusion*. Oxford: Oxford University Press.

Cahill, M. (1992). Personal mobility and social inequality. In P. Carter, T. Jeffs and M. K. Smith (eds), *Changing Social Work and Welfare*. Buckingham: Open University Press.

Cahill, M. (1994). *The New Social Policy*. Oxford: Blackwell.

Cairns, S., Sloman, L., Newson, C., Anable, J., Kirkbride, A. and Goodwin, P. (2004). *Smarter Choices: Changing the Way we Travel*. London: Department for Transport.

Campion, J., Greenhalgh, C. and Knight, J. (2003). *Mind the Gap: Leonard Cheshire's Social Exclusion Report 2003*. London: Leonard Cheshire.

Carrabine, E. and Longhurst, B. (2002). Consuming the car. *Sociological Review*, 50(2): 181–96.

Carter, N. and Ockwell, D. (2007). *New Labour, New Environment: An Analysis of the Labour Government's Policy on Climate Change and Biodiversity Loss*. London: Friends of the Earth.

Cass, N., Shove, E. and Urry, J. (2005). Social exclusion, mobility and access. *Sociological Review*, 53(3): 539–55.

Cavill, N. (2007). *Building Health: Creating and Enhancing Places for Healthy, Active Lives*. London: National Heart Forum.

Cavill, N. and Davis, A. (2007). *Cycling and Health: What's the Evidence?* London: Cycling England.

Centre for Transport Studies, Imperial College, Mott MacDonald and Institute for Transport Studies, University of Leeds (2006). *Social Inclusion: Transport Aspects*: London: Department for Transport.

Church, A. and Frost, M. (2000). Transport and Social Exclusion in London. *Transport Policy*, 7(3): 195–205.

Clement, B. (2006). The big question: are speed cameras really the best way to improve road safety? *The Independent*, 16 June.

Cole-Hamilton, I., Harrop, A. and Street, C. (2002). *The Value of Children's Play and Play Provison: A Systematic Review of the Literature*. London: New Policy Institute.

Commission for Integrated Transport (2004). *The Bus Industry: Encouraging Local Delivery*. London: Commission for Integrated Transport.

Commission for Integrated Transport (2007). *Transport and Climate Change*. London: Commission for Integrated Transport.

Commission for Integrated Transport (2008). *A New Approach to Rural Public Transport*. London: Commission for Integrated Transport.

Corbett, C. (2003). *Car Crime*. Cullompton: Willan.

Craig, G., Burchardt, T. and Gordon, D. (eds) (2008). *Social Justice and Public Policy*. Bristol: Policy Press.

Craig, R. and Mindell, J. (2006). *Health Survey for England 2006: Cardiovascular Disease and Risk Factors. Summary of key findings*. London: NHS Information Centre.

Crow, G. and Allan, G. (1994). *Community Life: An Introduction to Local Social Relations*. London: Harvester Wheatsheaf.

Cryer, C. (2001). *What Works to Prevent Accidental Injury amongst Older People*. Canterbury: University of Kent.

Dant, T. (2004). The driver-car. *Theory, Culture and Society*, 21(4/5): 61–79.

Davey, J. (2007). Older people and transport: coping without a car. *Ageing and Society*, 27: 49–65.

Davis, A., Valsecchi, C. and Fergusson, M. (2007). *Unfit for Purpose: How Car Use Fuels Climate Change and Obesity*. London: Institute for European Environmental Policy.

Davis, R. (1992). *Death on the Street: Cars and the Mythology of Road Safety*. Hawes: Leading Edge.

Dean, H. (2006). *Social Policy*. Cambridge: Polity Press.

Dean, J. S. (1947). *Murder Most Foul: A Study of the Road Deaths Problem*. London: George Allen & Unwin. Reprinted 2007.

Dennis, K. and Urry, J. (2009). *After the Car*. Cambridge: Polity Press.

Dennis, N., Henriques, F. and Slaughter, C. (1956). *Coal is Our Life: An Analysis of a Yorkshire Mining Community*. London: Eyre & Spottiswood.

Department for Children, Schools and Families (2007). *Children's Plan*. London: DCSF.

Department for Children, Schools and Families (2008). *Fair Play*, consultation document. London: DCSF.

Department for the Environment, Food and Rural Affairs (2007). *The Air Quality Strategy for England, Scotland, Wales and Northern Ireland*. London: Defra.

Department of the Environment, Transport and the Regions (1998). *A New Deal for Transport: Better for Everyone*. London: DETR.

Department of the Environment, Transport and the Regions (1999). *Towards an Urban Renaissance*. London: The Stationery Office.

Department of the Environment, Transport and the Regions (2001). *Planning Policy Guidance 13: Transport*. London: DETR.

Department of Health (1993). *The Health of the Nation*. London: DoH.

Department of Health (1995). *More People, More Active, More Often: Physical Activity in England*, consultation paper. London: DoH.

Department of Health (1998). *Our Healthier Nation*. London: DoH.

Department of Health (2001). *National Service Framework for Older People*. London: DoH.

Department of Health (2004). *Choosing Health: Making Healthy Choices Easier*. London: DoH.

Department of Health (2005). *Choosing Activity*. London: DoH.

Department of Health (2008). *Healthy Weight, Healthy Lives*. London: DoH.

Department of Transport (1996). *National Cycling Strategy*. London: DoT.

Department for Transport (2003a). *The Future of Air Transport*. London: DfT.

Department for Transport (2003b). *On the Move by Foot*, discussion paper.

Department for Transport (2004). *Walking and Cycling: An Action Plan*. London: DfT.

Department for Transport (2005a). *Home Zones: Challenging the Future of our Streets*. London: DfT.

Department for Transport (2005b). *National Travel Survey 2004*. London: DfT.

Department for Transport (2006a). *Accessibility Planning Guidance: Full Guidance*. London: DfT.

Department for Transport (2006b). *National Travel Survey 2005*. London: DfT.

Department for Transport (2006c). *Young People and Transport: Understanding their Needs and Requirements*. London: DfT Mobility and Inclusion Unit.

Department for Transport (2006d). *Road Casualties Great Britain 2005*. London: DfT.

Department for Transport (2007a). *Annual Report*. London: DfT.

Department for Transport (2007b). *Child Road Safety Strategy*. London: DfT.

Department for Transport (2007c). *Manual for Streets*. London: DfT.

Department for Transport (2007d). *National Travel Survey 2006*. London: DfT.

Department for Transport (2008a). *Delivering a Sustainable Transport System*. London: DfT.

Department for Transport (2008b). *National Travel Survey 2007*. London: DfT.

Department for Transport (2008c). *Transport Statistics Great Britain 2008*. London: DfT.

Department for Transport (2009a). *A Safer Way: Consultation on Making Britain's Roads the Safest in the World*. London: DfT.

Department for Transport (2009b). *Low Carbon Transport: A Greener Future*. London: DfT.

Department for Transport (2009c). *Transport Trends: 2008 Edition*. London: DfT.

Department of Transport, Local Government and the Regions (2000). *Women and Public Transport: The Checklist*. London: DTLR.

Docherty, I. and Shaw, J. (eds) (2003). *A New Deal for Transport?* Oxford: Blackwell.

Docherty, I. and Shaw, J. (eds) (2008). *Traffic Jam: Ten years of 'Sustainable' Transport in the UK*. Bristol: Policy Press.

Docherty, I., Shaw, J. and Gray, D. (2007). Transport strategy in Scotland since devolution. *Public Money and Management*, April: 141–8.

Dorling, D., Rigby, J., Wheeler, B., et al. (2007). *Poverty, Wealth and Place in Britain, 1968 to 2005*. Bristol: Policy Press/Joseph Rowntree Foundation.

DPTAC (Disabled Persons Transport Advisory Committee) (2002). *Attitudes of Disabled People to Public Transport: Research Study*. London: DPTAC. http://www.dptac.gov.uk/research/apt/03.htm (accessed July 2009).

Dunbar, G., Holland, C. A. and Maylor, E. A. (2004). *Older Pedestrians: A Critical Review of the Literature*. London: Department for Transport.

Dyos, H. J. and Aldcroft, D. H. (1973). *British Transport: An Economic Survey from the Seventeenth Century to the Twentieth*. London: Penguin.

Easterbrook, L., Horton, K., Arber, S. and Davidson, K. (2002). *International Review of Interventions in Falls among Older People*. London Department for Trade and Industry.

Eddington, R. (2006). *The Eddington Transport Study*. London: HM Treasury.

Edwards, P., Roberts, I., Green, J. and Lutchmun, S. (2006). Deaths from injury in children and employment status in family: analysis of trends in class specific death rates. *British Medical Journal*, 333(119).

Edwards, T. (2000). *Contradictions of Consumption*. Buckingham: Open University Press.

European Commission (1992). *The Future Development of the Common Transport Policy* (COM (92) 494). Brussels: European Commission.

European Commission (2001). *European Transport Policy for 2010: Time to Decide* (COM (2001) 370). Brussels: European Commission.

European Commission (2006). *Keep Europe moving – Sustainable mobility for our continent – Mid-term review of the European Commission's 2001 Transport White Paper* (SEC (2006) 768). Brussels: European Commission.

Foley, J. and Fergusson, M. (2003). *Putting the Brakes on Climate Change*. London: Institute for Public Policy Research.

Foresight (2007). *Tackling Obesities: Future Choices*, project report. London: Government Office for Science.

Fraser, D. (1976). *Urban Politics in Victorian England*. Leicester: Leicester University Press.

Freund, P. (2001). Bodies, disability and spaces: the social model and disabling spatial organizations. *Disability and Society*, 16(5): 689–706.

Freund, P. and Martin, G. (2004). Walking and motoring: fitness and the social organisation of movement. *Sociology of Health and Illness*, 26(3): 273–86.

Frumkin, H., Frank, L. and Jackson, R. (2004). *Urban Sprawl and Public Health*. Washington, DC: Island.

Gehl, J. (2001). *Life between Buildings: Using Public Space*. Copenhagen: Danish Architectural Press.

Giddens, A. (2009). *The Politics of Climate Change*. Cambridge: Polity Press.

Gilbert, R. and Perl, A. (2008). *Transport Revolutions: Moving People and Freight without Oil*. London: Earthscan.

Gilhooly, M., Hamilton, K. and O'Neill, M. (2002). *Transport and Ageing: Extending Quality of Life for Older People via Public and Private Transport*. Swindon: ESRC.

Gill, T. (2005). *Cycling and Children and Young People: A Review*. London: National Children's Bureau.

Gill, T. (2007). *Can I Play Out . . .? Lessons from London Play's Home Zones Project*. London: London Play.

Glaister, S., Burnham, J., Stevens, H. and Travers, T. (2006). *Transport Policy in Britain*, 2nd edn. Basingstoke: Palgrave Macmillan.

Goldthorpe, J., Lockwood, D., Bechhoffer, F. and Platt, J. (1968). *The Affluent Worker*. Cambridge: Cambridge University Press.

Goodwin, P., Hallett, S., Kenny, F. and Stokes, G. (1991). *Transport: The New Realism*. Oxford: Transport Studies Unit, University of Oxford.

Grahame, K. (1908). *The Wind in the Willows*. London: Methuen.

Grant, J. (1977). *The Politics of Urban Transport Planning*. London: Earth Resources Research.

Gray, D., Shaw, J. and Farrington, J. (2006). Community transport, social capital and social exclusion in rural areas. *Area*, 38(1): 89–98.

Grayling, T., Hallam, K., Graham, D., Anderson, R. and Glaister, S. (2002). *Streets Ahead: Safe and Liveable Streets for Children*. London: Institute for Public Policy Research.

Grayling, T., Sansom, N. and Foley, J. (2004). *In the Fast Lane: Fair and Effective Road User Charging in Britain*. London: Institute for Public Policy Research.

Greed, C. (2003). *Inclusive Urban Design: Public Toilets*. Oxford: Architectural Press.

Greed, C. (2008). Planning the non-sexist city: the Euro Fem initiative and beyond. *The Guardian*, 23 September.

Green, J. and Edwards, P. (2008). The limitations of targeting to address inequalities in health: a case study of road traffic injury prevention from the UK. *Critical Public Health*, 18(2): 175–87.

Grieco, M. (1995). Time pressures and low-income families: the implications for 'social' transport policy in Europe. *Community Development Journal*, 30(4): 347–63.

Hackett, G. (2007). All work, no play at Blair flagship school. *The Times*, 6 May.

Hajer, M. (1995). *The Politics of Environmental Discourse*. Oxford: Oxford University Press.

Halpern, D. (2005). *Social Capital*. Cambridge: Polity Press.

Hamer, M. (1987). *Wheels within Wheels*. London Routledge.

Hamilton, K., Jenkins, L., Hodgson, F. and Turner, J. (2005). *Promoting Gender Equality in Transport*. London: Equal Opportunities Commission.

Hart, J. (2008). Driven to excess: impacts of motor vehicle traffic on residential quality of life in Bristol, UK. Unpublished MsC thesis, University of the West of England, Bristol.

Hart, R. (1987). *The Changing City of Childhood: Implications for Play and Learning*. New York: City University of New York.

Help the Aged (2007). *Local Bus Services and Travel Concessions: Experiences and Views of Older People*. London: Help the Aged.

Help the Aged (2008). *Keeping on the Move*. London: Help the Aged.

Hillman, M., Adams, J. and Whitelegg, J. (1990). *One False Move . . . A Study of Children's Independent Mobility*. London: Policy Studies Institute.

Hillman, M. and Fawcett, T. (2004). *How We Can Save the Planet*. London: Penguin.

Hine, J. (2008). Social justice. In R. Knowles, J. Shaw and I. Docherty (eds), *Transport Geographies: Mobilities, Flows and Spaces*. Oxford: Blackwell.

Hirsch, F. (1976). *Social Limits to Growth*. Cambridge, Mass.: Harvard University Press.

Holland, C., Clark, A., Katz, J. and Peace, S. (2007). *Social Interventions in Urban Public Places*. Bristol: Joseph Rowntree Foundation/Policy Press.

Hopkins, R. (2008). *The Transition Handbook: From Oil Dependency to Local Resilience*. Dartington: Green Books.

House of Commons Environmental Audit Committee (2006). *Reducing Carbon Emissions from Transport*. London: The Stationery Office.

Huby, M. and Bradshaw, J. (2006). *A Review of the Environmental Dimension of Children and Young People's Well-being*. York: University of York.

Illich, I. (1974). *Energy and Equity*. London Calder & Boyars.

Imrie, R. (1998). Oppresson, disability and access in the built environment. In T. Shakespeare (ed.), *The Disability Reader: Social Science Perspectives*. London: Continuum.

Jacobs, J. (1962). *The Death and Life of Great American Cities*. London: Jonathan Cape.

Jain, J. and Guiver, J. (2001). Turning the car inside out: transport, equity and environment. *Social Policy and Administration*, 35(5): 569–86.

Jolly, D., Priestley, M. and Matthews, B. (2006). *Secondary Analysis of Exisiting Data on Disabled People's Use of and Experiences of Public Transport in Great Britain*. Leeds: University of Leeds.

Jones, A., Bentham, G., Foster, C., Hilldson, M. and Panter, J. (2007). *Tackling Obesities: Future Choices. Obesogenic Environments: Evidence Review*. London: Foresight Programme, Office for Science.

Jones, L. (1996). Putting transport on the social policy agenda. In M. May, E. Brunsdon and G. Craig (eds), *Social Policy Review 8*. London: Social Policy Association.

Kegerreis, S. (1993). Independent mobility and children's mental and emotional development. In M. Hillman (ed.), *Children, Transport and the Quality of Life*. London: Policy Studies Institute.

Kelly, R. (2008). Speech to Labour Party Conference, 24 September. http://www.labour.org.uk/ruth_kelly_speech,2008-09-24 (accessed July 2009).

Kenyon, S., Lyons, G. and Rafferty, J. (2002). Transport and social exclusion: investigating the possibility of promoting inclusion through virtual mobility. *Journal of Transport Geography*, 10: 207–19.

Kenyon, S., Lyons, G. and Rafferty, J. (2003). Social exclusion and transport: a role for virtual accessibility in the alleviation of mobility-related social exclusion? *Journal of Social Policy*, 32: 317–38.

King, R., Warnes, T. and Williams, A. (2000). *Sunset Lives: British Retirement Migration to the Mediterranean*. Oxford: Berg.

Knight, T., Dixon, J., Warrener, M. and Webster, S. (2007). *Understanding the Travel Needs, Behaviour and Aspirations of People in Later Life*. London: DfT.

Larsen, J., Urry, J. and Axhausen, K. (2006). *Mobilities Networks, Geographies*. Aldershot: Ashgate Press.

Layard, R. and Dunn, J. (2009). *A Good Childhood: Searching for Values in a Competitive Age*. London: Penguin.

Legge, K., Magadi, M., Phung, V-H. et al. (2006). *New Deal for Disabled People*. London: Department for Work and Pensions.

Little, J. (1994). *Gender, Planning and the Policy Process*. Oxford: Pergamon Press.

Lorenzoni, I., Nicholson-Cole, S. and Whitmarsh, L. (2007). Barriers perceived to engaging with climate change among the UK public and their policy implications. *Global Environmental Change*, 17(3/4): 445–59.

Lucas, K. (2004). *Running on Empty: Transport, Social Exclusion and Environmental Justice*. Bristol: Policy Press.

Lucas, K., Tyler, S. and Christodoulou, G. (2008). *The Value of New Transport in Deprived Areas*. York: Joseph Rowntree Foundation.

Lyons, G. (2003). Transport and society. Unpublished inaugural lecture, University of the West of England.

Mackett, R. L. (2001). Are we making our children car dependent? Lecture given at Trinity College, Dublin, 17 May 2001. Available at http://www.ucl.ac.uk/transport-studies/chcaruse.htm.

Mackinnon, D. and Vigar, G. (2008). Devolution and the UK's new policy landscape. In I. Docherty and J. Shaw (eds), *Traffic Jam: Ten Years of 'Sustainable' Transport in the UK*. Bristol: Policy Press.

Madanipur, A., Cars, G. and Allen, J. (1998). *Social Exclusion in European Cities*. London: Jessica Kingsley.

Marshall, T. H. and Bottomore, T. (1992). *Citizenship and Social Class*. London: Pluto Press.

McMillan, M. (1930). *The Nursery School*. London: Dent.

Merriman, P. (2007). *Driving Spaces*. Oxford: Blackwell.

Metz, D. (2003). Transport policy for an ageing population. *Transport Reviews*, 23(4): 375–86.

Metz, D. (2008). *The Limits to Travel: How Far Will you Go?* London: Earthscan.

Michael, M. (2001). The invisible car: the cultural purification of road rage. In D. Miller (ed.), *Car Cultures*. Oxford: Berg.

Miller, D. (2005). What is social justice? In N. Pearce and W. Paxton (eds), *Social Justice: Building a Fairer Britain*. London: IPPR/Politicos.

Millward, L. M., Morgan, A. and Kelly, M. P. (2003). *Prevention and Reduction of Accidental Injury in Children and Young People*. London: Health Development Agency.

Milmo, D. (2009). UK road deaths fall to record low. *The Guardian*, 25 June.

Moss, P. and Petrie, P. (2002). *From Children's Services to Children's Spaces*. London: Routledge Falmer.

Naess, P. (2008). Gender differences in the influences of urban structure on daily travel. In T. Priya Uteng and T. Cresswell (eds), *Gendered Mobilities*. Aldershot: Ashgate Press.

Nantulya, V. M. and Reich, M. R. (2002). The neglected epidemic: road traffic injuries in developing countries. *British Medical Journal*, 324(7346): 1139–41.

New Economics Foundation (n.d.). Ghost town Britain. http://www.neweconomics.org.uk/gen/local_ghost.aspx?page=960&folder=148& (accessed July 2009).

NHS Information Centre (2006). *Health Survey for England 2004. Updating of trend tables to include childhood obesity data*. http://www.ic.nhs.uk/pubs/hsechildobesityupdate (accessed July 2009).

Nussbaum, M. (2000). *Women and Human Development*. Cambridge: Cambridge University Press.

O'Connell, S. (1998). *The Car in British Society: Class, Gender and Motoring 1896–1939*. Manchester: Manchester University Press.

O'Connell, S. (2006). From Toad of Toad Hall to the 'Death Drivers' of Belfast. *British Journal of Criminology*, 46: 455–69.

O'Reilly, K. (2000). *The British on the Costa del Sol*. London: Routledge.

OECD (Organization for Economic Cooperation and Development) (2001). *Ageing and Transport: Mobility Needs and Safety Issues*. Paris: OECD.

Offer, A. (2006). *The Challenge of Affluence*. Oxford: Oxford University Press.

Office of the Deputy Prime Minister (2004). *Living Places: Caring for Quality*. London: ODPM.

Office for National Statistics (2005). *Focus on Personal Travel 2005*. London: ONS.

Office for National Statistics (2007). *Homicide in Scotland 2006–7*. London: ONS.

Oldenburg, R. (1999). *The Great Good Place*. New York: Marlowe.

Ouvry, M. (2003). *Exercising Muscles and Minds*. London: National Children's Bureau.

Parkhurst, G. and Dudley, G. (2008). Roads and traffic from 'predict and provide' to 'making best use'. In I. Docherty and J. Shaw (eds), *Traffic Jam: Ten Years of 'Sustainable' Transport in the UK*. Bristol: Policy Press.

Parliamentary Office of Science and Technology (2002). *Air Quality in the UK*. London: Parliamentary Office of Science and Technology.

Paterson, M. (2007). *Automobile Politics: Ecology and Cultural Political Economy*. Cambridge: Cambridge University Press.

Plowden, W. (1971). *The Motor Car and Politics 1896–1970*. London: The Bodley Head.

Plunkett, J. (2005). Scrap 'Top Gear', say road safety campaigners. *The Guardian*, 12 April.

Pooley, C., Turnbull, J. and Adams, M. (2005). *A Mobile Century? Changes in Everyday Mobility in Britain in the Twentieth Century*. Aldershot: Ashgate Press.

Pugh, M. (2008). *'We danced all night': A Social History of Britain between the Wars*. London: The Bodley Head.

Putnam, R. (2000). *Bowling Alone: The Collapse and Revival of American Community*. New York: Simon & Schuster.

Rabbitt, P., Carmichael, A., Shilling, V. and Sutcliffe, P. (2002). *Age, Health and Driving*. Manchester: University of Manchester/AA Foundation for Road Safety Research.

Raje, F. (2004). *Transport, Demand Management and Social Inclusion: The Need for Ethnic Perspectives*. Aldershot: Ashgate Press.

Redshaw, S. (2008). *In the Company of Cars: Driving as a Social and Cultural Practice*. Aldershot: Ashgate Press.

Reid Howie Associates (2000). *Women and Transport: Moving Forward*. Edinburgh: Scottish Executive.

Reilly, J. J., Kelly, L., Montgomery, C. et al. (2006). Physical activity to prevent obesity in young children: cluster randomised controlled trial. *British Medical Journal*, 333: 1041–5.

Roberts, I. (2001). Evidence based road safety: the Driving Standards Agency's schools programme. *The Lancet*, 358: 230–2.

Roberts, J., Cleary, J., Hamilton, K. and Hanna, J. (1992). *Travel Sickness: The Need for a Sustainable Transport Policy for Britain*. London: Lawrence & Wishart.

Roberts, J. T. and Parks, B. C. (2007). *A Climate of Injustice: Global Inequality, North–South Politics, and Climate Change*. Cambridge, MA: MIT Press.

Roberts, P. (2005). *The End of Oil*. London: Bloomsbury.

Rogers, R. (1997). *Cities for a Small Planet*. Boulder, Colo.: Westview Press.

Root, A. (2007). *Market Citizenship: Experiments in Democracy and Globalization*. London: Sage.

Rowntree, S. (2000 [1901]). *Poverty: A Study of Town Life*. Bristol: Policy Press.

Royal Commission on Environmental Pollution (2007). *The Urban Environment* London: The Stationery Office.

Schöppe, S. and Braubach, M. (2007). *Tackling Obesity by Creating Healthy Residential Environments*. Copenhagen: World Health Organization.

Searle, B. (2008). *Well-being: In Search of a Good Life?* Bristol: Policy Press.

Seebohm, F. (1968). *Report of the Committee on Local Authority and Allied Personal Socal Services* (Seebohm Report), Cmnd 3703. London: HMSO.

Sen, A. (1995). *Inequality Re-examined*. Oxford: Oxford University Press.

Sevenhuijsen, S. (1998). *Citizenship and the Ethics of Care*. London: Routledge.

Shaw, J. and Docherty, I. (2008). New deal or no new deal? A decade of 'sustainable' transport in the UK. In I. Docherty and J. Shaw (eds), *Traffic Jam: Ten Years of 'Sustainable' Transport in the UK*. Bristol: Policy Press.

Sheller, M. (2003). Automotive emotions: feeling the car. *Theory, Culture and Society*, 21(4/5): 221–42.

Sheller, M. and Urry, J. (2006). The new mobilities paradigm. *Environment and Planning A*, 38: 207–26.

Sherlock, H. (1991). *Cities are Good for Us*. London: Paladin.

Sloman, L. (2006). *Car Sick: Solutions for our Car-addicted Culture*. Dartington: Green Books.

Slower Speeds Initiative (2000). *Speed Kills*. Hereford: Slower Speeds Initiative.

Smith, N., Beckhelling, J., Ivaldi, A., Kellard, K., Sandu, A. and Tarrant, C. (2006). *Evidence Base Review on Mobility: Choices and Barriers for Different Social Groups*, No. CRSP 554. Loughborough: Centre for Research in Social Policy, University of Loughborough.

Social Exclusion Unit (2003). *Making the Connections: Final Report on Transport and Social Exclusion*. London: The Stationery Office.

Solomon, J. (1998). *To Drive or to Vote? Young Adults' Culture and Priorities*. London: The Chartered Institute of Transport.

Soule, A., Babb, P., Evandrou, M. and Sealey, L. (2005). *Focus on Older People*. London: Office for National Statistics.

Spicker, P. (2007). *The Idea of Poverty*. Bristol: Policy Press.

Spicker, P. (2008). *Social Policy: Themes and Approaches*. Bristol: Policy Press.

Stacey, M. (1960). *Tradition and Change: A study of Banbury*. Oxford: Oxford University Press.

Stacey, M., Batstone, E., Bell, C. and Muscott, A. (1975). *Power, Persistence and Change: A Second Study of Banbury*. London: Routledge & Kegan Paul.

Steer Davies Gleave (2006) *Driving up Carbon Dioxide Emissions from Road Transport: An Analysis of Current Government Projections*. London: Transport 2000.

Stevens, H. (2004). *Transport Policy in the European Union*. London: Palgrave Macmillan.

Stradling, S., Anable, J., Anderson, T. and Cronberg, A. (2008) Car use and climate change: do we practise what we preach? In A. Park et al. (eds), *British Social Attitudes: the 24th Report*. London: Sage/National Centre for Social Research.

Sustainable Development Commission (2007). *Every Child's Future Matters*. London: Sustainable Development Commission.

Sustrans (2007a). *Creating the Environment for Active Travel*. Bristol: Sustrans.

Sustrans (2007b). *The National Cycle Network Route User Monitoring Report*. Bristol: Sustrans.

Sustrans (2008). *Active Travel and Healthy Workplaces*. Bristol: Sustrans.

Sutton, C. (2008). Women get in gear for the buying process. *Real Business*, 23 April. http://www.realbusiness.co.uk/columnists/clive-sutton/5242086/women-get-in-gear-for-the-buying-process.thtml (accessed July 2009).

Swinford, S. (2009). UK tops league for toxic traffic fumes. *Sunday Times*, 1 March.

Tanne, J. H. (2004). Walking protects elderly people from dementia, studies show. *British Medical Journal*, 329(7469): 761.

Taylor, I. and Sloman, L. (2008). *Towards Transport Justice: Transport and Social Justice in an Oil-Scarce Future*. Machynlleth: Transport for Quality of Life.

Thomsen, T. U. (2004). Children – Automobility's Immobilized Others? *Transport Reviews*, 24(5): 515–32.

Tolley, R. (2003). *Sustainable Transport*. Cambridge: Woodhead Publishing.

Townsend, P. (1979). *Poverty in the United Kingdom*. Harmondsworth: Penguin.

Transport and Health Study Group (1991). *Health on the Move: Policies for Health-Promoting Transport*. Birmingham: Public Health Alliance.

Transport for London (2004). *Expanding Horizons: Transport for London's Women's Action Plan 2004*. London: TfL.

Transport for London (2008). *Cycling in London*. London: TfL.

Transport for London (n.d.). Congestion charging. http://www.tfl.gov.uk/roadusers/congestioncharging/6723.aspx (accessed July 2009).

Travis, A. (2008). Murder rate falls for fifth successive year but concern over 'hidden' family violence. *The Guardian*, 1 February.

Twigg, J. (2006). *The Body in Health and Social Care*. Basingstoke: Palgrave Macmillan.

UK Noise Association (2007). *Traffic Noise – a problem, but there are solutions.* Available at www.ukna.org.uk.

Unicef (2007). *An Overview of Child Well-being in Rich Countries: A Comprehensive Assessment of the Lives and Well-being of Children and Adolescents.* Florence: Unicef.

Urry, J. (2000). *Sociology beyond Societies.* London: Routledge.

Urry, J. (2002). Mobility and proximity. *Sociology*, 36(2): 255–74.

Urry, J. (2007). *Mobilities.* Cambridge: Polity Press.

Valentine, G. (2004). *Public Space and the Culture of Childhood.* Aldershot: Ashgate Press.

Vanderbilt, T. (2008). *Traffic: Why We Drive the Way We Do (And What It Says About Us).* London: Allen Lane.

Vidal, J. (2009). Europe to prosecute Britain for breaking air pollution laws. *The Guardian*, 29 January.

Vigar, G. (2002). *The Politics of Mobility: Transport, the Environment and Public Policy.* London: Spon Press.

Wanless, D. (2004). *Securing Good Health for the Whole Nation* (Wanless Report). London: The Stationery Office.

Ward, C. (1978). *The Child in the City.* London: Architectural Press.

Ward, L. (2008). Life through a lens: how Britain's children eat, sleep and breathe TV. *The Guardian*, 16 January.

Wardman, J., Tight, M. and Page, M. (2007). Factors influencing the propensity to cycle to work. *Transportation Research Part A*, 41: 339–50.

Webster, D., Tilly, A., Nicholls, D. and Buttress, S. (2006). *Pilot Home Zones Schemes: Summary of the Schemes.* London: TRL for the Department for Transport.

Webster, L. and Shah, S. (2008). *Into the Unknown: Disabled People's Experiences of Public.* London: Leonard Cheshire.

White, P. (2009). *Public Transport: Its Planning, Management and Operation.* London: Routledge.

Whitelegg, J. and Cambridge, H. (2004). *Aviation and Sustainability.* Stockholm: Stockholm Environment Institute.

Whitelegg, J. and Haq, G. (2006). *Vision Zero: Adopting a Target of Zero for Road Traffic Fatalities and Serious Injuries.* London: Stockholm Environment Institute.

Wickham, J. (2006a). *Gridlock: Dublin's Transport Crisis and the Future of the City.* Dublin: New Island Press.

Wickham, J. (2006b). Public transport systems: the sinews of European urban citizenship. *European Societies*, 8(1): 3–26.

Willmott, P. and Thomas, D. (1984). *Community in Social Policy.* London: Policy Studies Institute.

Wilson, L-M. (2003). *An Overview of the Literature on Disability and Transport.* London: Disability Rights Commission.

Wolff, J. and De-Shalit, A. (2007). *Disadvantage.* Oxford: Oxford University Press.

Wolmar, C. (2007). *Fire and Steam: How the Railways Transformed Britain.* London: Atlantic Books.

World Health Organization (2000). *Air Quality and Health.* http://www.who.int/mediacentre/factsheets/fs313/en/index.html (accessed July 2009).

World Health Organization (2004a). *Transport Related Health Effects with a Particular Focus on Children*. Vienna: WHO Europe.

World Health Organization (2004b). *World Report on Road Traffic Injury Prevention*. Geneva: WHO.

World Health Organization (2008). *World Report on Child Injury Prevention*. Geneva: WHO.

Young, M. and Willmott, P. (1957). *Family and Kinship in East London*. London: Routledge & Kegan Paul.

Zarb, G. (ed.) (1995). *Removing Disabling Barriers*. London: Policy Studies Institute.

Index

Related books from Open University Press
Purchase from www.openup.co.uk or order through your local bookseller

---

REVISITING THE WELFARE STATE
Robert Page

- What was the impact of the Second World War on the development of the welfare state?
- Did Attlee's pioneering post-war Labour governments create the welfare state and a socialist society?
- Was there a welfare consensus between Labour and the Conservatives in the period from 1951 to 1979?
- Was there a welfare revolution during the Thatcher and Major years?
- What lies at the heart of New Labour's welfare policy?

In *Revisiting the Welfare State*, Robert Page provides a persuasive, fresh and challenging account of the British welfare state since 1940. His text re-examines some of the most commonly held assumptions about the post-war welfare state and reignites the debate about its role and purpose.

Robert Page starts from the premise that the student of social policy can gain a deeper understanding of the welfare state by studying political and historical accounts of the welfare state, party manifestos, policy documents and political memoirs. Drawing from these sources, he provides a clear guide to the changing role of the state in the provision of welfare since 1940. Each of the five chapters is devoted to a particular theme associated with the post-war welfare state, the last of which focuses on the strategy of the New Labour governments of Tony Blair.

Written by one of the leading authorities on contemporary social policy, *Revisiting the Welfare State* is a stimulating guide to the political history of the post-war welfare state in Britain. It is essential reading for students of social policy, social work, politics and contemporary history. It will also appeal to the general reader who is seeking an accessible guide to the political history of the post-war welfare state.

Contents
Series editor's foreword – Acknowledgements – List of abbreviations – Introduction – The impact of war on the 'Home' Front, the coalition government and the Welfare State – Revisiting the Labour Governments 1945–1951: towards a Democratic Socialist Welfare State and society? – Revisiting the Welfare State from 1951–1979: an era of consensus in social policy? – Revisiting the Conservative welfare 'revolution': the Thatcher and Major years 1979–1997 – Revisiting New Labour and the Welfare State – Bibliography – Index

2007   176pp
978-0-335-21317-7 (Paperback)   978-0-335-21318-4 (Hardback)

POLICY
THIRD EDITION

H. K. Colebatch

This third edition of Hal Colebatch's book, *Policy*, is a welcome addition to the policy literature. Through a series of interrelated questions–such as Why worry about policy? What is it for? What does it look like on the ground? and How do we do it? – Colebatch interestingly unravels and elaborates on the key issues, both practical and theoretical, that constitute the field of policy studies. In a very succinct and highly readable style, the nine chapters weave together discussions of traditional models and approaches (e.g., process models, rationality, and incrementalism) with a presentation of newer emphases (e.g., social constructivism, discourse, and his own innovative concept of 'policy work'). He does it in ways that are accessible to the beginning university student, but that are, at the same time, helpful to the experienced practitioner. As such, the book is highly recommendable.

Professor Frank Fischer, Rutgers University, USA

This new edition of a highly successful text provides an even sharper critical analysis than before of the place of policy in the way we are governed. It is a book about policy – not about what governments do ('public policy') or about particular fields of policy (such as 'health policy' or 'education policy') but about policy as a concept – an idea which makes sense of the way in which we are governed, and which we can use to be more effective participants in this governing.

Policy is key reading for the student studying the subject, the public official or community activist engaged in making policy, and the interested member of the public who wants to know where policy comes from, and why it matters.

Contents
Preface – Acknowledgements – Why Worry About It? – What's the Idea? – What's Going On? – What Is It For? – What Else Is There? – What Do They Say About It? – What Does It Look Like on the Ground? – How Do You Do It? – Where Do We Go from Here? – Bibliography – Index.

2008   184pp
978-0-335-23547-9 (Paperback)

RACE AND EDUCATION
POLICY AND POLITICS IN BRITAIN

Sally Tomlinson

This book is an extremely useful tool for understanding the ways in which discrimination within education are realised, as well as the issues and policies that facilitate it.

Children & Young People Now

- How successful has Britain been in accommodating racial, religious and cultural diversity in the education system?
- Have there been contradictory policies that have encouraged migrant labour, while urging immigration control?
- Has the introduction of market principles to education created further problems for ethnic minorities?

This book provides crucial information on key educational issues, events and conflicts in Britain from the 1960s to the present day, as the education system has attempted to incorporate racial and ethnic minorities and educate young people to live in an ethnically diverse society. It uses examples such as political and media reactions to Afro hairstyles in the 1970s through to hijabs and niquabs today, to illustrate how misplaced are the simplistic arguments that blame multiculturalism or minorities for segregation or lack of community cohesion.

Race and Education: Policy and Politics in Britain describes how over the decades schools, teachers, parents, local communities and local authorities have worked towards the incorporation of minority children into the education system. It asserts that negative and contradictory policies by governments and a continued climate of hostility to those variously labelled as immigrant, ethnic minority, or non-white has made this extremely difficult.

The book sets educational issues and events within a wider social and political context, taking account of national and global influences, and changing political beliefs and actions over the years. Sally Tomlinson argues that debates needs to focus less on dress and more on the educational, housing and employment problems, symptomatic of the continued poverty in many minority areas that works against social cohesion.

Race and Education: Policy and Politics in Britain is an invaluable resource for all those concerned with education and social policy, especially students and professionals working in education, sociology and social policy.

Contents
Series editor's foreword – Acknowledgements – List of abbreviations – Introduction – Assimilation aspirations (1960–1970) – Post-imperial anxieties (1970–1980) – Race, riots and markets (1980–1990) – The absent presence (1990–1997) – Summary

2008   248pp
978-0-335-2-2307-7(Paperback)   978-0-335-2-2308-4 (Hardback)